Exercises for

A Canadian Writer's Reference

Seventh Edition

Diana Hacker

Nancy Sommers
Harvard University

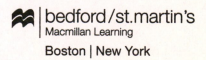

bedford/st.martin's
Macmillan Learning

Boston | New York

For information, write: Bedford/St. Martin's, 75 Arlington Street, Boston, MA 02116

ISBN 978-1-319-19184-9

21098 fedcb

A Note for Instructors

The exercise sets in this collection are keyed to specific sections in *A Canadian Writer's Reference*. You are welcome to photocopy any or all of these exercises for a variety of possible uses:

- as homework
- as classroom practice
- as quizzes
- as individualized self-teaching assignments
- as support for a writing center or learning lab

Most exercise sets begin with an example that is done for the student, followed by five lettered sentences. This resource also includes paragraph-style editing exercises. Answers and possible revisions are given in a separate PDF file that will be available for download from the Macmillan catalogue page for *A Canadian Writer's Reference*, Seventh Edition. If you would like students to work independently, checking all of their revisions themselves, you may of course reproduce the answer key.

Contents

Sentence Style

Word Choice

Grammatical Sentences

Multilingual Writers and ESL Topics

Punctuation and Mechanics

Basic Grammar

Exercise S1-1 ◆ Parallelism

Before working this exercise, read section S1 in *A Canadian Writer's Reference*, Seventh Edition.

Edit the following sentences to correct faulty parallelism. Possible revisions appear in the answer key. Example:

>   *checking*
> **Rowena began her workday by pouring a cup of coffee and ~~checked~~ her email.**
>   ^

a.   Police dogs are used for finding lost children, tracking criminals, and the detection of bombs and illegal drugs.

b.   Hannah told her rock-climbing partner that she bought a new harness and of her desire to climb Mount McConnell.

c.   It is more difficult to sustain an exercise program than starting one.

d.   During basic training, I was not only told what to do but also what to think.

e.   Jan wanted to drive to the wine country or at least the Niagara Escarpment.

Exercise S1-2 ◆ Parallelism

Before working this exercise, read section S1 in *A Canadian Writer's Reference*, Seventh Edition.

Revise the following paragraph to balance parallel ideas. A possible revision appears in the answer key.

Community service can provide tremendous benefits not only for the organization receiving the help but the volunteer providing the help, too. This dual benefit idea is behind a recent move to make community service hours a graduation requirement in high schools across the country. For many nonprofit organizations, seeking volunteers is often smarter financially than to hire additional employees. For many young people, community service positions can help develop empathy, being committed, and leadership. Opponents of the trend argue that volunteerism should not be mandatory, but research shows that community service requirements are keeping students engaged in school and lower dropout rates dramatically. Parents, school administrators, and people who are leaders in the community all seem to favour the new initiatives.

Hacker/Sommers, *Exercises for A Canadian Writer's Reference,*
7th ed. (Boston: Bedford, 2019)

Exercise S2-1 ◆ Needed words

Before working this exercise, read section S2 in *A Canadian Writer's Reference*, Seventh Edition.

Add any words needed for grammatical or logical completeness in the following sentences. Possible revisions appear in the answer key. Example:

> that
> The officer feared the prisoner would escape.
> ^

a. A grapefruit or orange is a good source of vitamin C.

b. The women entering the military academy can expect haircuts as short as the male cadets.

c. Looking out the family room window, Sarah saw her favourite tree, which she had climbed as a child, was gone.

d. The graphic designers are interested and knowledgeable about producing posters for the balloon race.

e. The Great Barrier Reef is larger than any coral reef in the world.

Exercise S3-1 ◆ Misplaced modifiers

Before working this exercise, read sections S3-a to S3-d in *A Canadian Writer's Reference*, Seventh Edition.

Edit the following sentences to correct misplaced or awkwardly placed modifiers. Possible revisions appear in the answer key. Example:

> *in a phone survey*
> **Answering questions can be annoying. ~~in a phone survey.~~**
>   ^   ^

a. More research is needed to effectively evaluate the risks posed by volcanoes in the Pacific Northwest.

b. Many students graduate with debt from university totalling more than twenty thousand dollars.

c. It is a myth that humans only use 10 percent of their brains.

d. A coolhunter is a person who can find in the unnoticed corners of modern society the next wave of fashion.

e. All geese do not fly beyond Kamloops for the winter.

Hacker/Sommers, *Exercises for A Canadian Writer's Reference,*
7th ed. (Boston: Bedford, 2019)

Exercise S3-2 ◆ Dangling modifiers

Before working this exercise, read section S3-e in *A Canadian Writer's Reference*, Seventh Edition.

Edit the following sentences to correct dangling modifiers. Most sentences can be revised in more than one way. Possible revisions appear in the answer key. Example:

> *a student must complete*
> **To acquire a degree in almost any field, two science courses. must be completed.**
> ^   ^

a.   To complete an online purchase with a credit card, the expiration date and the security

      code must be entered.

b.   Though only sixteen, UBC accepted Martha's application.

c.   Settled in the cockpit, the pounding of the engine was muffled only slightly by my helmet.

d.   After studying polymer chemistry, computer games seemed less complex to Phuong.

e.   When a young man, my mother enrolled me in tap dance classes.

Exercise S4-1 ◆ Shifts: Point of view

Before working this exercise, read section S4-a in *A Canadian Writer's Reference*, Seventh Edition.

Edit the following paragraph to eliminate distracting shifts in point of view (person and number). Create two versions. First, imagine that this is an introductory paragraph designed to engage the reader with a personal story; write it in the first person (using *I* and *we*). Can you think of other contexts in which the first-person point of view would be the best choice? Then write the paragraph in the third person (using *people* and *they*). In what contexts would this version be the best choice? Possible revisions appear in the answer key.

When online dating first became available, many people thought that it would simplify romance. We believed that you could type in a list of criteria—sense of humour, postsecondary education, green eyes, good job—and a database would select the perfect mate. Thousands of people signed up for services and filled out their profiles, confident that true love was only a few mouse clicks away. As it turns out, however, virtual dating is no easier than traditional dating. I still have to contact the people I find, exchange emails and phone calls, and meet him in the real world. Although a database might produce a list of possibilities and screen out obviously undesirable people, you can't predict chemistry. More often than not, people who seem perfect online just don't click in person. Electronic services do help a single person expand their pool of potential dates, but it's no substitute for the hard work of romance.

Hacker/Sommers, *Exercises for A Canadian Writer's Reference*, 7th ed. (Boston: Bedford, 2019)

Exercise S4-2 ◆ Shifts: Tense

Before working this exercise, read section S4-b in *A Canadian Writer's Reference*, Seventh Edition.

Edit the following paragraphs to eliminate distracting shifts in tense. Possible revisions appear in the answer key.

Settling Canada was arduous. Until 1608, many European attempts at permanent settlements — at Sable Island, Tadoussac, and Port Royal, for example — failed.

The first successful settlement begins on July 3, 1608, when Samuel de Champlain founded Quebec for France. Although Champlain formed an alliance with the Algonquian and Montagnais peoples, survival is still difficult. To help his settlers develop skills, Champlain sends men to live with the Aboriginal peoples. These men were known as the *coureurs de bois* (runners of the woods).

Twenty-eight people had originally settled Quebec. By 1630, the number had risen to only one hundred. The *coureurs de bois* extend the French influence to the Huron peoples in the Great Lakes area, but the English colonies were stronger. To bolster the French colony, in 1627 Cardinal Richelieu, regent of France, founded the Company of 100 Associates. He gives land to people to settle in New France and names Champlain governor.

Champlain was a prolific writer. He spent 1629 to 1632 writing a seven-hundred-page book called Les *voyages de la nouvelle France*. In his works, Champlain reveals nothing about himself; his meticulous descriptions of what he did and saw contained no value judgments and opinions. Thus his works were the best account we had of the beginnings of Canadian history.

Hacker/Sommers, *Exercises for A Canadian Writer's Reference,*
7th ed. (Boston: Bedford, 2019)

S4-2 | Shifts: Tense   **7**

Exercise S4-3 ◆ Shifts: Mood and voice, questions and quotations

Before working this exercise, read sections S4-c and S4-d in *A Canadian Writer's Reference*, Seventh Edition.

Edit the following sentences to make the verbs consistent in mood and voice and to eliminate distracting shifts from indirect to direct questions or quotations. Possible revisions appear in the answer key. Example:

> **As a public relations intern, I wrote press releases, managed the website, and**
> fielded all phone calls.
> ~~all phone calls were fielded by me.~~
>   ^

a. A talented musician, Julie Crochetière uses R&B, soul, and jazz styles. Even pop music is performed well by her.

b. Environmentalists point out that shrimp farming in Southeast Asia is polluting water and making farmlands useless. They warn that action must be taken by governments before it is too late.

c. The samples were observed for five days before we detected any growth.

d. In his famous soliloquy, Hamlet contemplates whether death would be preferable to his difficult life and, if so, is he capable of committing suicide?

e. The lawyer told the judge that Miranda Hale was innocent and allow her to prove the allegations false.

Hacker/Sommers, *Exercises for A Canadian Writer's Reference,*
7th ed. (Boston: Bedford, 2019)

Exercise S4-4 ◆ Shifts

Before working this exercise, read section S4 in *A Canadian Writer's Reference*, Seventh Edition.

Edit the following sentences to eliminate distracting shifts. Possible revisions appear in the answer key. Example:

> **For many first-year engineering students, the course load can be so rigorous that ~~you~~ sometimes feel overwhelmed.**
>
> *they*

a.   A courtroom lawyer needs to have more than a touch of theatre in their blood.

b.   The interviewer asked whether we had brought our proof of citizenship and did we bring our passports?

c.   The experienced reconnaissance scout knows how to make fast decisions and use sophisticated equipment to keep their team from being detected.

d.   After the animators finish their scenes, the production designer arranges the clips according to the storyboard. Synchronization notes must also be made for the sound editor and the composer.

e.   Madame Defarge is a sinister figure in Dickens's *A Tale of Two Cities*. On a symbolic level, she represents fate; like the Greek Fates, she knitted the fabric of individual destiny.

Hacker/Sommers, *Exercises for A Canadian Writer's Reference*, 7th ed. (Boston: Bedford, 2019)

S4-4 | Shifts   **9**

Exercise S5-1 ◆ Mixed constructions

Before working this exercise, read section S5 in *A Canadian Writer's Reference*, Seventh Edition.

Edit the following sentences to untangle mixed constructions. Possible revisions appear in the answer key. Example:

> Taking
> ~~By taking~~ the oath of citizenship made Ling a Canadian citizen.
> ^

a.   Using surgical gloves is a precaution now worn by dentists to prevent contact with

patients' blood and saliva.

b.   A physician, the career my brother is pursuing, requires at least ten years of challenging

work.

c.   The reason the pharaohs had bad teeth was because tiny particles of sand found their way

into Egyptian bread.

d.   Recurring bouts of flu among team members set a record for number of games forfeited.

e.   In this box contains the key to your future.

Hacker/Sommers, *Exercises for A Canadian Writer's Reference,*
7th ed. (Boston: Bedford, 2019)

Exercise S6-1 ◆ Coordination and subordination

Before working this exercise, read section S6-a in *A Canadian Writer's Reference*, Seventh Edition.

Use the coordination or subordination technique in brackets to combine each pair of independent clauses. Possible revisions appear in the answer key. Example:

> baseball, but he
> **Ferguson Jenkins** was one of the best pitchers in the history of ~~baseball. He~~ never won
> a **World Series ring.** [*Use a comma and a coordinating conjunction.*]

a. In 1987, Jenkins was elected to the Canadian Baseball Hall of Fame. He was the first Canadian elected to the Baseball Hall of Fame in Cooperstown, New York. [*Use a comma and a coordinating conjunction.*]

b. Jenkins was the first Canadian pitcher to win the Cy Young Award. He also won the Lou Marsh Trophy as Canada's outstanding athlete in 1974. [*Use a semicolon.*]

c. Jenkins was grateful to have won the Cy Young Award. Jenkins felt that he should have won more awards. [*Use the subordinating conjunction* although.]

d. Jenkins loved being a baseball pitcher. He told *Baseball Almanac* that he didn't consider pitching to be work. [*Use a semicolon and the transitional phrase* for example.]

e. In the last forty years, Jenkins is the only Major League pitcher with six straight twenty-win seasons. He will likely be the last pitcher to do it because today's pitchers start fewer games. [*Use a semicolon.*]

Hacker/Sommers, *Exercises for A Canadian Writer's Reference*,
7th ed. (Boston: Bedford, 2019)

S6-1 | Coordination and subordination   **11**

Exercise S6-2 ◆ Coordination and subordination

Before working this exercise, read section S6-b in *A Canadian Writer's Reference*, Seventh Edition.

Combine the following sentences by subordinating minor ideas or by coordinating ideas of equal importance. You must decide which ideas are minor because the sentences are given out of context. Possible revisions appear in the answer key. Example:

> **Agnes, ~~was~~ a girl I worked with/, ~~She~~ was a hyperactive child.**

a.   The X-Men comic books and Japanese woodcuts of kabuki dancers were part of Marlena's research project on popular culture. They covered the tabletop and the chairs.

b.   Our waitress was costumed in a kimono. She had painted her face white. She had arranged her hair in a lacquered beehive.

c.   Students can apply for a spot in the leadership program. The program teaches thinking and communication skills.

d.   Shore houses were flooded up to the first floor. Beaches were washed away. Brant's Lighthouse was swallowed by the sea.

e.   Laura Thackray was an engineer at Volvo Car Corporation. She addressed women's safety needs. She designed a pregnant crash-test dummy.

Hacker/Sommers, *Exercises for A Canadian Writer's Reference,*
7th ed. (Boston: Bedford, 2019)

Exercise S6-3 ◆ Coordination and subordination

Before working this exercise, read sections S6-a and S6-c in *A Canadian Writer's Reference*, Seventh Edition.

The following sentences show coordinated ideas (ideas joined with a coordinating conjunction or a semicolon). Restructure the sentences by subordinating minor ideas. You must decide which ideas are minor because the sentences are given out of context. Possible revisions appear in the answer key. Example:

> The rowers returned to shore, ~~and~~ had a party on the beach ~~and celebrated~~ *where they* ... *to celebrate*
>
> the start of the season.

a. These particles are known as "stealth liposomes," and they can hide in the body for a long time without detection.

b. Irena is a competitive gymnast and majors in biochemistry; her goal is to apply her athletic experience and her science degree to a career in sports medicine.

c. Students, textile workers, and labour unions have loudly protested sweatshop abuses, so apparel makers have been forced to examine their labour practices.

d. IRC (internet relay chat) was developed in a European university; it was created as a way for a group of graduate students to talk about projects from their dorm rooms.

e. The cafeteria's new menu has an international flavour, and it includes everything from enchiladas and pizza to pad thai and sauerbraten.

Hacker/Sommers, *Exercises for A Canadian Writer's Reference*, 7th ed. (Boston: Bedford, 2019)

S6-3 | Coordination and subordination **13**

Exercise S6-4 ◆ Faulty subordination

Before working this exercise, read sections S6-d and S6-e in *A Canadian Writer's Reference*, Seventh Edition.

In each of the following sentences, the idea that the writer wished to emphasize is buried in a subordinate construction. Restructure each sentence so that the independent clause expresses the major idea, as indicated in brackets, and lesser ideas are subordinated. Possible revisions appear in the answer key. Example:

> Although
> **Catherine has weathered many hardships, ~~although~~ she has rarely become**
> ^
> **discouraged.** [*Emphasize that Catherine has rarely become discouraged.*]

a.   Gina worked as an aide for the relief agency, distributing food and medical supplies.

   [*Emphasize distributing food and medical supplies.*]

b.   Janbir spent every Saturday learning tabla drumming, noticing with each hour of

   practice that his memory for complex patterns was growing stronger. [*Emphasize Janbir's*

   memory.]

c.   The rotor hit, gouging a hole about five millimetres deep in my helmet. [*Emphasize that the*

   rotor gouged a hole in the helmet.]

d.   My grandfather, who raised his daughters the old-fashioned way, was born eighty years

   ago in Puerto Rico. [*Emphasize how the grandfather raised his daughters.*]

e.   The Narcan reversed the depressive effect of the drug, saving the patient's life. [*Emphasize*

   that the patient's life was saved.]

14   S6-4 | Faulty subordination

Hacker/Sommers, *Exercises for A Canadian Writer's Reference,*
7th ed. (Boston: Bedford, 2019)

Exercise S7-1 ◆ Sentence variety

Before working this exercise, read section S7 in *A Canadian Writer's Reference*, Seventh Edition.

Improve sentence variety in each of the following sentences by using the technique suggested in brackets. Possible revisions appear in the answer key. Example:

> To protect endangered marine turtles, fishing
> ~~Fishing~~ crews place turtle excluder devices in fishing nets. ~~to protect endangered~~
> ^
> ~~marine turtles.~~ [*Begin the sentence with the adverbial infinitive phrase.*]

a. The exhibits for insects and spiders are across the hall from the fossils exhibit. [*Invert the sentence.*]

b. Sayuri becomes a successful geisha after growing up desperately poor in Japan. [*Move the adverb phrase to the beginning of the sentence.*]

c. Researchers have been studying Mount St. Helens for years. They believe that a series of earthquakes in the area may have caused the 1980 eruption. [*Combine the sentences into a complex sentence. See also B4-a.*]

d. Ice cream typically contains 10 percent milk fat. Premium ice cream may contain up to 16 percent milk fat and has considerably less air in the product. [*Combine the two sentences as a compound sentence.*]

e. The economy may recover more quickly than expected if home values climb. [*Move the adverb clause to the beginning of the sentence.*]

Hacker/Sommers, *Exercises for A Canadian Writer's Reference,*
7th ed. (Boston: Bedford, 2019)

S7-1 | Sentence variety   **15**

Exercise S7-2 ◆ Sentence variety

Before working this exercise, read section S7 in *A Canadian Writer's Reference*, Seventh Edition.

Edit the following paragraph to increase sentence variety. A possible revision appears in the answer key.

Making architectural models is a skill that requires patience and precision. It is an art that illuminates a design. Architects come up with a grand and intricate vision. Draftspersons convert that vision into blueprints. The model maker follows the blueprints. The model maker builds a miniature version of the structure. Modellers can work in traditional materials like wood and clay and paint. Modellers can work in newer materials like Styrofoam and liquid polymers. Some modellers still use cardboard, paper, and glue. Other modellers prefer glue guns, deformable plastic, and thin aluminum and brass wire. The modeller may seem to be making a small mess in the early stages of model building. In the end the modeller has completed a small-scale structure. Architect Rem Koolhaas has insisted that plans reveal the logic of a design. He has argued that models expose the architect's vision. The model maker's art makes this vision real.

Hacker/Sommers, *Exercises for A Canadian Writer's Reference,*
7th ed. (Boston: Bedford, 2019)

Exercise W2-1 ◆ Wordy sentences

Before working this exercise, read section W2 in *A Canadian Writer's Reference*, Seventh Edition.

Edit the following sentences to reduce wordiness. Possible revisions appear in the answer key. Example:

> even though
> The Wilsons moved into the house ~~in spite of the fact that~~ the back door was only
> ^
> ten metres from the train tracks.

a. Martin Luther King Jr. was a man who set a high standard for future leaders to meet.

b. Alice has been deeply in love with cooking since she was little and could first peek over the edge of a big kitchen tabletop.

c. In my opinion, Bloom's race to be premier is a futile exercise.

d. It is pretty important in being a successful graphic designer to have technical knowledge and at the same time an eye for colour and balance.

e. Your task will be the delivery of correspondence to all employees in the company.

Hacker/Sommers, *Exercises for A Canadian Writer's Reference,*
7th ed. (Boston: Bedford, 2019)

W2-1 | Wordy sentences **17**

Exercise W2-2 ◆ Wordy sentences

Before working this exercise, read section W2 in *A Canadian Writer's Reference*, Seventh Edition.

Edit the following business memo to reduce wordiness. A possible revision appears in the answer key.

To: District managers

From: Margaret Davenport, Vice President

Subject: Customer database

It has recently been brought to my attention that a percentage of our sales representatives have been failing to log reports of their client calls in our customer database each and every day. I have also learned that some representatives are not checking the database on a routine basis.

Our clients sometimes receive a multiple number of sales calls from us when a sales representative is not cognizant of the fact that the client has been contacted at a previous time. Repeated telephone calls from our representatives annoy our customers. These repeated telephone calls also portray our company as one that is lacking in organization.

Effective as of immediately, direct your representatives to do the following:

- Record each and every customer contact in the customer database at the end of each day, without fail.
- Check the database at the very beginning of each day to ensure that telephone communications will not be initiated with clients who have already been called.

Let me extend my appreciation to you for cooperating in this important matter.

Hacker/Sommers, *Exercises for A Canadian Writer's Reference,*
7th ed. (Boston: Bedford, 2019)

Exercise W3-1 ◆ Active verbs

Before working this exercise, read section W3 in *A Canadian Writer's Reference*, Seventh Edition.

Revise any weak, unemphatic sentences by replacing passive verbs or *be* verbs with active alternatives. You may need to name in the subject the person or thing doing the action. If a sentence is already emphatic, do not change it. Possible revisions appear in the answer key. Example:

> The warden doused the campfire before giving us
> ~~The campfire was doused by the warden before we were given~~ a ticket for unauthorized
> ^
> use of a campsite.

a.   The Prussians were victorious over the Saxons in 1745.

b.   The entire operation is managed by Ahmed, the producer.

c.   The sea kayaks were expertly paddled by the tour guides.

d.   At the crack of rocket and mortar blasts, I jumped from the top bunk and landed on my

buddy below, who was crawling on the floor looking for his boots.

e.   There were shouting protesters on the courthouse steps.

Exercise W3-2 ◆ Active verbs

Before working this exercise, read section W3 in *A Canadian Writer's Reference*, Seventh Edition.

For each writing situation below, decide whether it is more appropriate to use the active voice or the passive voice. Answers appear in the answer key.

a.   You are writing a research paper explaining the effects of a deadly bacterial outbreak in a remote Chilean village. (active / passive)

b.   You are writing a letter to the editor, praising an emergency medical technician whose quick action saved an injured motorist. (active / passive)

c.   You are writing a summary of the procedure you used in an experiment for your biology class. (active / passive)

d.   To accompany your résumé, you must write a cover letter explaining your recent accomplishments as a manager. (active / passive)

e.   You must fill out an incident report, explaining in detail how your actions led to a collision between the forklift you were operating and a wall of fully stocked shelves. (active / passive)

Hacker/Sommers, *Exercises for A Canadian Writer's Reference,*
7th ed. (Boston: Bedford, 2019)

Exercise W4-1 ◆ Jargon and pretentious language

Before working this exercise, read sections W4-a and W4-b in *A Canadian Writer's Reference*, Seventh Edition.

Edit the following sentences to eliminate jargon, pretentious or flowery language, euphemisms, and doublespeak. You may need to make substantial changes in some sentences. Possible revisions appear in the answer key. Example:

> After two weeks in the legal department, Sue has ~~worked into~~ *mastered* the routine, ~~of the office,~~ *office* and her ~~functional and self-management skills have~~ *performance has* exceeded all expectations.

a. In my youth, my family was under the constraints of difficult financial circumstances.

b. In order that I may increase my expertise in the area of delivery of services to clients, I feel that participation in this conference will be beneficial.

c. The prophetic meteorologist cautioned the general populace regarding the possible deleterious effects of the impending tempest.

d. Governmentally sanctioned investigations into the continued value of after-school programs indicate a perceived need in the public realm at large.

e. Passengers should endeavour to finalize the customs declaration form prior to exiting the aircraft.

Exercise W4-2 ◆ Jargon

Before working this exercise, read sections W4-a and W4-b in *A Canadian Writer's Reference*, Seventh Edition.

Edit the following email message to eliminate jargon. A possible revision appears in the answer key.

Dear Ms. Jackson:

We members of the Nakamura Reyes team value our external partnering arrangements with Creative Software, and I look forward to seeing you next week at the trade show in Vancouver. Per Mr. Reyes, please let me know when you'll have some downtime there so that he and I can conduct a strategizing session with you concerning our production schedule. It's crucial that we all be on the same page re our 2017–2018 product release dates.

Before we have some face time, however, I have some findings to share. Our customer-centric approach to the new products will necessitate that user testing periods trend upward. The enclosed data should help you effectuate any adjustments to your timeline; let me know ASAP if you require any additional information to facilitate the above.

Before we convene in Vancouver, Mr. Reyes and I will agendize any further talking points. Thanks for your help.

Sincerely,

Sylvia Nakamura

Hacker/Sommers, *Exercises for A Canadian Writer's Reference,*
7th ed. (Boston: Bedford, 2019)

Exercise W4-3 ◆ Slang and level of formality

Before working this exercise, read sections W4-d and W4-e in *A Canadian Writer's Reference*, Seventh Edition.

Revise the following passage twice. First, use a level of formality appropriate for a newspaper editorial directed toward a general audience. Then use a level of formality appropriate for a blog post directed at young adults. Possible revisions appear in the answer key.

In pop culture, college or university grads who return home to live with the folks are seen as good-for-nothing losers who mooch off their families. And many older adults seem to feel that the trend of moving back home after school, which was rare in their day, is becoming too commonplace today. But society must realize that a cultural shift is taking place. Most young adults want to live on their own ASAP, but they graduate with heaps of debt and need some time to become financially stable. College or university tuition and the cost of housing have increased way more than salary increases in the past half century. Also, the job market is tighter and more jobs require advanced degrees than in the past. So before people go off on college and university graduates who move back into their parents' house for a spell, they must indeed consider all the facts.

Hacker/Sommers, *Exercises for A Canadian Writer's Reference*,
7th ed. (Boston: Bedford, 2019)

W4-3 | Slang and level of formality   **23**

Exercise W4-4 ◆ Nonsexist language

Before working this exercise, read section W4-f in *A Canadian Writer's Reference*, Seventh Edition.

Edit the following sentences to eliminate sexist language or sexist assumptions. Possible revisions appear in the answer key. Example:

> *Scholarship athletes*   *their*   *they are*
> ~~A scholarship athlete~~ must be as concerned about ~~his~~ academic performance as ~~he is~~
>   *their*
> about ~~his~~ athletic performance.

a.　Mrs. Geralyn Farmer, who is the mayor's wife, is the chief surgeon at University Hospital. Dr. Paul Green is her assistant.

b.　Every applicant wants to know how much he will earn.

c.　An elementary school teacher should understand the concept of nurturing if she intends to be effective.

d.　An obstetrician needs to be available to his patients at all hours.

e.　If man does not stop polluting his environment, mankind will perish.

Hacker/Sommers, *Exercises for A Canadian Writer's Reference*, 7th ed. (Boston: Bedford, 2019)

Exercise W4-5 ◆ Nonsexist language

Before working this exercise, read section W4-f in *A Canadian Writer's Reference*, Seventh Edition.

Eliminate sexist language or sexist assumptions in the following job posting for an elementary school teacher. A possible revision appears in the answer key.

We are looking for qualified women for the position of elementary school teacher. The ideal candidate should have a bachelor's degree, a teaching certificate, and one year of student teaching. She should be knowledgeable in all elementary subject areas, including science and math. While we want our new teacher to have a commanding presence in the classroom, we are also looking for motherly characteristics such as patience and trustworthiness. She must be able to both motivate an entire classroom and work with each student one-on-one to assess his individual needs. She must also be comfortable communicating with the parents of her students. For salary and benefits information, including maternity leave policy, please contact the Upper Canada District School Board. Any qualified applicant should submit her résumé by March 15.

Hacker/Sommers, *Exercises for A Canadian Writer's Reference*, 7th ed. (Boston: Bedford, 2019)

W4-5 | Nonsexist language **25**

Exercise W5-1 ◆ Synonyms

Before working this exercise, read section W5-a in *A Canadian Writer's Reference*, Seventh Edition.

Use a dictionary and a thesaurus to find at least four synonyms for each of the following words. Be prepared to explain any slight differences in meaning.

1.   decay (verb)

2.   difficult (adjective)

3.   hurry (verb)

4.   pleasure (noun)

5.   secret (adjective)

6.   talent (noun)

Hacker/Sommers, *Exercises for A Canadian Writer's Reference,*
7th ed. (Boston: Bedford, 2019)

Exercise W5-2 ◆ Misused words

Before working this exercise, read section W5-c in *A Canadian Writer's Reference*, Seventh Edition.

Edit the following sentences to correct misused words. Possible revisions appear in the answer key. Example:

> all-absorbing.
> **These days the training required for a ballet dancer is ~~all-absorbent.~~**
>   ^

a. We regret this delay; thank you for your patients.

b. Ada's plan is to require education and experience to prepare herself for a position as property manager.

c. Serena Williams, the penultimate competitor, has earned millions of dollars just in endorsements.

d. Many people take for granite that public libraries have up-to-date computer systems.

e. The affect of Gao Xingjian's novels on Chinese exiles is hard to gauge.

Exercise W5-3 ◆ Standard idioms

Before working this exercise, read section W5-d in *A Canadian Writer's Reference*, Seventh Edition.

Edit the following sentences to eliminate errors in the use of idiomatic expressions. If a sentence is correct, write "correct" after it. Possible revisions appear in the answer key. Example:

> by
> **We agreed to abide ~~with~~ the decision of the judge.**
> ^

a.   Queen Anne was so angry at Sarah Churchill that she refused to see her again.

b.   Jean-Pierre's ambitious travel plans made it impossible for him to comply with the

residency requirement for the graduate program.

c.   The parade moved off of the street and onto the beach.

d.   The frightened refugees intend on making the dangerous trek across the mountains.

e.   What type of a wedding are you planning?

Hacker/Sommers, *Exercises for A Canadian Writer's Reference,*
7th ed. (Boston: Bedford, 2019)

Exercise W5-4 ◆ Clichés and mixed figures of speech

Before working this exercise, read sections W5-e and W5-f in *A Canadian Writer's Reference*, Seventh Edition.

Edit the following sentences to replace worn-out expressions and clarify mixed figures of speech. Possible revisions appear in the answer key. Example:

> *the color drained from his face.*
> **When he heard about the accident, ~~he turned white as a sheet.~~**
>   ^

a.   John stormed into the room like a bull in a china shop.

b.   Some people insist that they'll always be there for you, even when they haven't been before.

c.   The Blue Jays easily beat the Mets, who were in the soup early in the game today at the Rogers Centre.

d.   We ironed out the sticky spots in our relationship.

e.   My mother accused me of beating around the bush when in fact I was just talking off the top of my head.

Exercise G1-1 ◆ Subject-verb agreement

Before working this exercise, read section G1 in *A Canadian Writer's Reference*, Seventh Edition.

Edit the following sentences to eliminate problems with subject-verb agreement. If a sentence is correct, write "correct" after it. Answers appear in the answer key. Example:

> Jack's first days in the military ~~was~~ *were* gruelling.
>   ^

a. One of the main reasons for elephant poaching are the profits received from selling the ivory tusks.

b. Not until my interview with Dr. Hwang were other possibilities opened to me.

c. A number of students in the seminar was aware of the importance of joining the discussion.

d. Batik cloth from Bali, blue and white ceramics from Delft, and a bocce ball from Turin has made Angelie's room the talk of the dorm.

e. The board of directors, ignoring the wishes of the neighbourhood, has voted to allow further development.

Hacker/Sommers, *Exercises for A Canadian Writer's Reference*, 7th ed. (Boston: Bedford, 2019)

Exercise G1-2 ◆ Subject-verb agreement

Before working this exercise, read section G1 in *A Canadian Writer's Reference*, Seventh Edition.

For each sentence in the following passage, underline the subject (or compound subject) and then select the verb that agrees with it. (If you have trouble identifying the subject, consult B2-a.) Answers appear in the answer key.

Loggerhead sea turtles (migrate / migrates) thousands of kilometres before returning to their nesting location every two to three years. The nesting season for loggerhead turtles (span / spans) the hottest months of the summer. Although the habitat of Atlantic loggerheads (range / ranges) from Newfoundland to Argentina, nesting for these turtles (take / takes) place primarily along the southeastern coast of the United States. Female turtles that have reached sexual maturity (crawl / crawls) ashore at night to lay their eggs. The cavity that serves as a nest for the eggs (is / are) dug out with the female's strong flippers. Deposited into each nest (is / are) anywhere from fifty to two hundred spherical eggs, also known as a *clutch*. After a two-month incubation period, all eggs in the clutch (begin / begins) to hatch, and within a few days the young turtles attempt to make their way into the ocean. A major cause of the loggerhead's decreasing numbers (is / are) natural predators such as raccoons, birds, and crabs. Beach erosion and coastal development also (threaten / threatens) the turtles' survival. For example, a crowd of curious humans or lights from beachfront residences (is / are) enough to make the female abandon her nesting plans and return to the ocean. Since only one in one thousand loggerheads survives to adulthood, special care should be taken to protect this threatened species.

Hacker/Sommers, *Exercises for A Canadian Writer's Reference,*
7th ed. (Boston: Bedford, 2019)

G1-2 | Subject-verb agreement   **31**

Exercise G2-1 ◆ Irregular verbs

Before working this exercise, read section G2-a in *A Canadian Writer's Reference*, Seventh Edition.

Edit the following sentences to eliminate problems with irregular verbs. If a sentence is correct, write "correct" after it. Answers appear in the answer key. Example:

>   *saw*
> The warden ~~seen~~ the forest fire fifteen kilometres away.
>   ^

a. When I get the urge to exercise, I lay down until it passes.

b. Grandmother had drove our new hybrid to the sunrise church service, so we were left with the station wagon.

c. A pile of dirty rags was laying at the bottom of the stairs.

d. How did the game know that the player had went from the room with the blue ogre to the hall where the gold was heaped?

e. The computer programmer was an expert in online security; he was confident that the encryption code he used could never be broke.

Hacker/Sommers, *Exercises for A Canadian Writer's Reference,*
7th ed. (Boston: Bedford, 2019)

Exercise G2-2 ◆ -s and -ed verb endings and omitted verbs

Before working this exercise, read sections G2-c to G2-e in *A Canadian Writer's Reference*, Seventh Edition.

Edit the following sentences to eliminate problems with *-s* and *-ed* verb forms and with omitted verbs. If a sentence is correct, write "correct" after it. Answers appear in the answer key. Example:

>   *covers*
> **The Pell Grant sometimes ~~cover~~ the student's full tuition.**
>   ^

a.   The glass sculptures of the Swan Boats was prominent in the brightly lit lobby.

b.   Visitors to the glass museum were not suppose to touch the exhibits.

c.   Our church has all the latest technology, even a close-circuit television.

d.   Christos didn't know about Marlo's promotion because he never listens. He always talking.

e.   Most psychologists agree that no one performs well under stress.

Exercise G2-3 ◆ Verb tense and mood

Before working this exercise, read sections G2-f and G2-g in *A Canadian Writer's Reference*, Seventh Edition.

Edit the following sentences to eliminate errors in verb tense or mood. If a sentence is correct, write "correct" after it. Answers appear in the answer key. Example:

> *had been*
> After the path ~~was~~ plowed, we were able to walk in the park.
> ^

a. The palace of Knossos in Crete is believed to have been destroyed by fire around 1375 BCE.

b. Watson and Crick discovered the mechanism that controlled inheritance in all life: the workings of the DNA molecule.

c. When city planners proposed rezoning the waterfront, did they know that the mayor promised to curb development in that neighbourhood?

d. Tonight's concert begins at 9:30. If it was earlier, I'd consider going.

e. The math position was filled by the instructor who had been running the tutoring centre.

Hacker/Sommers, *Exercises for A Canadian Writer's Reference,*
7th ed. (Boston: Bedford, 2019)

Exercise G3-1 ◆ Pronoun-antecedent agreement

Before working this exercise, read section G3-a in *A Canadian Writer's Reference*, Seventh Edition.

Edit the following sentences to eliminate problems with pronoun-antecedent agreement. Most of the sentences can be revised in more than one way, so experiment before choosing a solution. If a sentence is correct, write "correct" after it. Possible revisions appear in the answer key. Example:

> Recruiters
> ~~The recruiter~~ may tell the truth, but there is much that they choose not to tell.
> ^

a.   Every candidate for prime minister must appeal to a wide variety of ethnic and social groups if they want to win the election.

b.   Either Tom Hanks or Harrison Ford will win an award for their lifetime achievement in cinema.

c.   The aerobics teacher motioned for everyone to move their arms in wide, slow circles.

d.   The parade committee was unanimous in its decision to allow all groups and organizations to join the festivities.

e.   The applicant should be bilingual if they want to qualify for this position.

Hacker/Sommers, *Exercises for A Canadian Writer's Reference*,
7th ed. (Boston: Bedford, 2019)

G3-1 | Pronoun-antecedent agreement   **35**

Exercise G3-2 ◆ Pronoun-antecedent agreement

Before working this exercise, read section G3-a in *A Canadian Writer's Reference*, Seventh Edition.

Edit the following paragraph to eliminate problems with pronoun-antecedent agreement or sexist language. A possible revision appears in the answer key.

A common practice in businesses is to put each employee in their own cubicle. A typical cubicle resembles an office, but their walls don't reach the ceiling. Many office managers feel that a cubicle floor plan has its advantages. Cubicles make a large area feel spacious. In addition, they can be moved around so that each new employee can be accommodated in his own work area. Of course, the cubicle model also has problems. Typically, an employee is not as happy with a cubicle as they would be with a traditional office. Also, productivity can suffer. Neither a manager nor a frontline worker can ordinarily do their best work in a cubicle because of noise and lack of privacy. Each worker can hear his neighbours tapping on computer keyboards, making telephone calls, and muttering under their breath.

Hacker/Sommers, *Exercises for A Canadian Writer's Reference*, 7th ed. (Boston: Bedford, 2019)

Exercise G3-3 ◆ Pronoun reference

Before working this exercise, read section G3-b in *A Canadian Writer's Reference*, Seventh Edition.

Edit the following sentences to correct errors in pronoun reference. In some cases, you will need to decide on an antecedent that the pronoun might logically refer to. Possible revisions appear in the answer key. Example:

> **Although Apple makes the most widely recognized tablet device, other companies have**
>
> *The competition*
> **gained a share of the market. ~~This~~ has kept prices from skyrocketing.**
> ^

a.   They say that engineering students should have hands-on experience with dismantling

and reassembling machines.

b.   She had decorated her living room with posters from chamber music festivals. This led

her date to believe that she was interested in classical music. Actually she preferred rock.

c.   In my high school, you didn't need to get all A's to be considered a success; you just

needed to work to your ability.

d.   Marianne told Jenny that she was worried about her mother's illness.

e.   Though Lewis cried for several minutes after scraping his knee, eventually it subsided.

Exercise G3-4 ◆ Pronoun reference

Before working this exercise, read section G3-b in *A Canadian Writer's Reference*, Seventh Edition.

Edit the following passage to correct errors in pronoun reference. In some cases, you will need to decide on an antecedent that the pronoun might logically refer to. A possible revision appears in the answer key.

Since its launch in the 1980s, the internet has grown to be one of the largest communications forums in the world. The internet was created by a team of academics who were building on a platform that government scientists had started developing in the 1950s. They initially viewed it as a noncommercial enterprise that would serve only the needs of the academic and technical communities. But with the introduction of user-friendly browser technology in the 1990s, it expanded tremendously. By the late 1990s, many businesses were connecting to the internet with high-speed broadband and fibre-optic connections, which is also true of home users today. Accessing information, shopping, gaming, and communicating are easier than ever before. This, however, can lead to some possible drawbacks. You forfeit privacy when you search, shop, game, and communicate. They say that avoiding disclosure of personal information and routinely adjusting your privacy settings on social media sites are the best ways to protect yourself on the internet.

Hacker/Sommers, *Exercises for A Canadian Writer's Reference*, 7th ed. (Boston: Bedford, 2019)

Exercise G3-5 ◆ Pronoun case: Personal pronouns

Before working this exercise, read section G3-c in *A Canadian Writer's Reference*, Seventh Edition.

Edit the following sentences to eliminate errors in pronoun case. If a sentence is correct, write "correct" after it. Answers appear in the answer key. Example:

> $\overset{he.}{}$
> **Grandfather cuts down trees for neighbours much younger than ~~him.~~**
> $\wedge$

a. Rick applied for the job even though he heard that other candidates were more experienced than he.

b. The volleyball team could not believe that the coach was she.

c. She appreciated him telling the truth in such a difficult situation.

d. The director has asked you and I to draft a proposal for a new recycling plan.

e. Five close friends and myself rented a station wagon, packed it with food, and drove two hundred kilometres to the Calgary Stampede.

Exercise G3-6 ◆ Pronoun case

Before working this exercise, read section G3-c in *A Canadian Writer's Reference*, Seventh Edition.

In the following paragraph, choose the correct pronoun in each set of parentheses. Answers appear in the answer key.

We may blame television for the number of products based on characters in children's TV shows—from Big Bird to SpongeBob—but in fact merchandising that capitalizes on a character's popularity started long before television. Raggedy Ann began as a child's rag doll, and a few years later books about (she / her) and her brother, Raggedy Andy, were published. A cartoonist named Johnny Gruelle painted a cloth face on a family doll and applied for a patent in 1915. Later Gruelle began writing and illustrating stories about Raggedy Ann, and in 1918 (he / him) and a publisher teamed up to publish the books and sell the dolls. He was not the only one to try to sell products linked to children's stories. Beatrix Potter published the first of many Peter Rabbit picture books in 1902, and no one was better than (she / her) at making a living from spin-offs. After Peter Rabbit and Benjamin Bunny became popular, Potter began putting pictures of (they / them) and their little animal friends on merchandise. Potter had fans all over the world, and she understood (them / their) wanting to see Peter Rabbit not only in books but also on teapots and plates and lamps and other furnishings for the nursery. Potter and Gruelle, like countless others before and since, knew that entertaining children could be a profitable business.

Hacker/Sommers, *Exercises for A Canadian Writer's Reference,*
7th ed. (Boston: Bedford, 2019)

Exercise G3-7 ◆ Pronoun case: *Who* and *whom*

Before working this exercise, read section G3-d in *A Canadian Writer's Reference*, Seventh Edition.

Edit the following sentences to eliminate errors in the use of *who* and *whom* (or *whoever* and *whomever*). If a sentence is correct, write "correct" after it. Answers appear in the answer key. Example:

>   *whom*
> **What is the address of the artist ~~who~~ Antonio hired?**

a.   Arriving late for rehearsal, we had no idea who was supposed to dance with whom.

b.   The environmental policy conference featured scholars who I had never heard of.

c.   Whom did you support in last month's election for student government president?

d.   Daniel always gives a holiday donation to whomever needs it.

e.   So many singers came to the audition that Natalia had trouble deciding who to select for the choir.

Exercise G4-1 ◆ Adjectives and adverbs

Before working this exercise, read section G4 in *A Canadian Writer's Reference*, Seventh Edition.

Edit the following sentences to eliminate errors in the use of adjectives and adverbs. If a sentence is correct, write "correct" after it. Possible revisions appear in the answer key. Example:

> *well*
> **We weren't surprised by how ~~good~~ the sidecar racing team flowed through the**
> **^**
>
> **tricky course.**

a.   Do you expect to perform good on the nursing board exam next week?

b.   With the budget deadline approaching, our office hasn't hardly had time to handle routine

     correspondence.

c.   When I worked in a flower shop, I learned that some flowers smell surprisingly bad.

d.   The customer complained that he hadn't been treated nice by the agent on the phone.

e.   Of all the smart people in my family, Uncle Roberto is the most cleverest.

Hacker/Sommers, *Exercises for A Canadian Writer's Reference*, 7th ed. (Boston: Bedford, 2019)

Exercise G4-2 ◆ Adjectives and adverbs

Before working this exercise, read section G4 in *A Canadian Writer's Reference*, Seventh Edition.

Edit the following passage to eliminate errors in the use of adjectives and adverbs. A possible revision appears in the answer key.

Doctors recommend that to give skin the most fullest protection from ultraviolet rays, people should use plenty of sunscreen, limit sun exposure, and wear protective clothing. The commonest sunscreens today are known as "broad spectrum" because they block out both UVA and UVB rays. These lotions don't feel any differently on the skin from the old UVA-only types, but they work best at preventing premature aging and skin cancer.

Many sunscreens claim to be waterproof, but they won't hardly provide adequate coverage after extended periods of swimming or perspiring. To protect good, even waterproof sunscreens should be reapplied liberal and often. All areas of exposed skin, including ears, backs of hands, and tops of feet, need to be coated good to avoid burning or damage. Some people's skin reacts bad to PABA, or para-aminobenzoic acid, so PABA-free (hypoallergenic) sunscreens are widely available. In addition to recommending sunscreen, doctors almost unanimously agree that people should stay out of the sun when rays are the most strongest—between 10:00 a.m. and 3:00 p.m.—and should limit time in the sun. They also suggest that people wear long-sleeved shirts, broad-brimmed hats, and long pants whenever possible.

Hacker/Sommers, *Exercises for A Canadian Writer's Reference,*
7th ed. (Boston: Bedford, 2019)

G4-2 | Adjectives and adverbs **43**

Exercise G5-1 ◆ Sentence fragments

Before working this exercise, read section G5 in *A Canadian Writer's Reference*, Seventh Edition.

Repair any fragment by attaching it to a nearby sentence or by rewriting it as a complete sentence. If a word group is correct, write "correct" after it. Possible revisions appear in the answer key. Example:

> One Greek island that should not be missed is Mykonos/, ^*a* A vacation spot for Europeans
>
> and a playground for the rich and famous.

a.   Listening to the CD her sister had sent, Mia was overcome with a mix of emotions.

      Happiness, homesickness, and nostalgia.

b.   Cortés and his soldiers were astonished when they looked down from the mountains and

      saw Tenochtitlán. The magnificent capital of the Aztecs.

c.   Although my spoken French is not very good. I can read the language with ease.

d.   There are several reasons for not eating meat. One reason being that dangerous chemicals

      are used throughout the various stages of meat production.

e.   To learn how to sculpt beauty from everyday life. This is my intention in studying art and

      archaeology.

Hacker/Sommers, *Exercises for A Canadian Writer's Reference,*
7th ed. (Boston: Bedford, 2019)

Exercise G5-2 ◆ Sentence fragments

Before working this exercise, read section G5 in *A Canadian Writer's Reference*, Seventh Edition.

Repair each fragment in the following passage by attaching it to a sentence nearby or by rewriting it as a complete sentence. A possible revision appears in the answer key.

Digital technology has revolutionized information delivery. Forever blurring the lines between information and entertainment. Yesterday's readers of books and newspapers are today's readers of e-books and blogs. Countless readers have moved on from print information entirely. Choosing instead to point, click, and scroll their way through a text online or on an e-reader. Once a nation of people spoon-fed television commercials and the six o'clock evening news. We are now seemingly addicted to YouTube and social media. Remember the family trip when Dad or Mom wrestled with a road map? On the way to Banff or Whistler? No wrestling is required with a GPS device. Unless it's Mom and Dad wrestling over who gets to program the address. Accessing information now seems to be Canada's favourite pastime. Statistics Canada, in its Canadian Internet Use Survey, reports that 80 percent of Canadian adults use the internet for personal reasons. Connecting mostly from home. As a country, we embrace information and communication technologies. Which now include, smartphones and tablets. Among children and adolescents, social media and other technology use are well established. For activities like socializing, gaming, and information gathering.

Hacker/Sommers, *Exercises for A Canadian Writer's Reference,*
7th ed. (Boston: Bedford, 2019)

G5-2 | Sentence fragments   **45**

Exercise G6-1 ◆ Run-on sentences

Before working this exercise, read section G6 in *A Canadian Writer's Reference*, Seventh Edition.

Revise the following run-on sentences using the method of revision suggested in brackets. Possible revisions appear in the answer key. Example:

> *Because*
> **Orville had been obsessed with his weight as a teenager, he rarely ate anything**
> ^
> **sweet.** [*Restructure the sentence.*]

a.   The city had one public swimming pool, it stayed packed with children all summer long. [*Restructure the sentence.*]

b.   The building is being renovated, therefore at times we have no heat, water, or electricity. [*Use a comma and a coordinating conjunction.*]

c.   The view was not what the travel agent had described, where were the rolling hills and the shimmering rivers? [*Make two sentences.*]

d.   Walker's coming-of-age novel is set against a gloomy scientific backdrop, the Earth's rotation has begun to slow down. [*Use a semicolon.*]

e.   City officials had good reason to fear a major earthquake, most of the business district was built on landfill. [*Use a colon.*]

Hacker/Sommers, *Exercises for A Canadian Writer's Reference,*
7th ed. (Boston: Bedford, 2019)

Exercise G6-2 ◆ Run-on sentences

Before working this exercise, read section G6 in *A Canadian Writer's Reference*, Seventh Edition.

Revise any run-on sentences using a technique that you find effective. If a sentence is correct, write "correct" after it. Possible revisions appear in the answer key. Example:

> **Crossing so many time zones on an eight-hour flight, I knew I would be tired when I
> arrived,** ~~**however,**~~ *but* **I was too excited to sleep on the plane.**

a. Wind power for the home is a supplementary source of energy, it can be combined with electricity, gas, or solar energy.

b. Aidan viewed Sofia Coppola's *Lost in Translation* three times and then wrote a paper describing the film as the work of a mysterious modern painter.

c. In the Middle Ages, the streets of London were dangerous places, it was safer to travel by boat along the Thames.

d. "He's not drunk," I said, "he's in insulin shock."

e. Are you able to endure extreme angle turns, high speeds, frequent jumps, and occasional crashes, then supermoto racing may be a sport for you.

Hacker/Sommers, *Exercises for A Canadian Writer's Reference,*
7th ed. (Boston: Bedford, 2019)

G6-2 | Run-on sentences **47**

Exercise G6-3 ◆ Run-on sentences

Before working this exercise, read section G6 in *A Canadian Writer's Reference*, Seventh Edition.

In the following rough draft, revise any run-on sentences. A possible revision appears in the answer key.

Some parents and educators argue that requiring uniforms in public schools would improve student behaviour and performance. They think that uniforms give students a more professional attitude toward school, moreover, they believe that uniforms help create a sense of community among students from diverse backgrounds. But parents and educators should consider the drawbacks to requiring uniforms in public schools.

Uniforms do create a sense of community, they do this, however, by stamping out individuality. Youth is a time to express originality, it is a time to develop a sense of self. One important way young people express their identities is through the clothes they wear. The self-patrolled dress code of high school students may be stricter than any school-imposed code, nevertheless, trying to control dress habits from above will only lead to resentment or to mindless conformity.

If children are going to act like adults, they need to be treated like adults, they need to be allowed to make their own choices. Telling young people what to wear to school merely prolongs their childhood. Requiring uniforms undermines the educational purpose of public schools, which is not just to teach facts and figures but to help young people grow into adults who are responsible for making their own choices.

Hacker/Sommers, *Exercises for A Canadian Writer's Reference,*
7th ed. (Boston: Bedford, 2019)

Exercise M1-1 ◆ Verb forms and tenses

Before working this exercise, read sections M1-a and M1-b in *A Canadian Writer's Reference*, Seventh Edition.

Revise the following sentences to correct errors in verb forms and tenses in the active and the passive voice. You may need to look at G2-a for the correct form of some irregular verbs and at G2-f for help with tenses. Answers appear in the answer key. Example:

> The meeting ~~begin~~ *begins* tonight at 7:30.

a.   In the past, tobacco companies deny any connection between smoking and health problems.

b.   The volunteer's compassion has touch many lives.

c.   I am wanting to register for a summer tutoring session.

d.   By the end of the year, the province will have test 139 birds for avian flu.

e.   The golfers were prepare for all weather conditions.

Hacker/Sommers, *Exercises for A Canadian Writer's Reference,*
7th ed. (Boston: Bedford, 2019)

M1-1 | Verb forms and tenses   **49**

Exercise M1-2 ◆ Verb forms with modals

Before working this exercise, read section M1-c in *A Canadian Writer's Reference*, Seventh Edition.

Edit the following sentences to correct errors in the use of verb forms with modals. If a sentence is correct, write "correct" after it. Answers appear in the answer key. Example:

We should ~~to~~ order pizza for dinner.

a.   A major league pitcher can to throw a baseball more than ninety-five miles per hour.

b.   The writing centre tutor will helps you revise your essay.

c.   A reptile must adjusted its body temperature to its environment.

d.   In some provinces, individuals may renew a driver's licence online.

e.   My uncle, a cartoonist, could sketched a face in less than a minute.

Hacker/Sommers, *Exercises for A Canadian Writer's Reference,*
7th ed. (Boston: Bedford, 2019)

Exercise M1-3 ◆ Negative verb forms and conditional verbs

Before working this exercise, read sections M1-d and M1-e in *A Canadian Writer's Reference*, Seventh Edition.

Edit the following sentences to correct problems with verbs. In some cases, more than one revision is possible. Possible revisions appear in the answer key. Example:

>   *had*
> **If I ~~have~~ time, I would study both French and Russian next semester.**
>   ^

a. The electrician might have discovered the broken circuit if she went through the modules one at a time.

b. If Verena wins a scholarship, she would go to graduate school.

c. Whenever a rainbow appears after a storm, everybody came out to see it.

d. Sarah did not understood the terms of her internship.

e. If I live in Budapest with my cousin Szusza, she would teach me Hungarian cooking.

Hacker/Sommers, *Exercises for A Canadian Writer's Reference*, 7th ed. (Boston: Bedford, 2019)

M1-3 | Negative verb forms and conditional verbs   **51**

Exercise M1-4 ◆ Verbs followed by gerunds or infinitives

Before working this exercise, read sections M1-d and M1-e in *A Canadian Writer's Reference*, Seventh Edition.

Form sentences by adding gerund or infinitive constructions to the following sentence openings. In some cases, more than one kind of construction is possible. Possible answers appear in the answer key. Example:

> **Please remind** your sister to call me.
> ^

a. I enjoy

b. The tutor told Samantha

c. The team hopes

d. Ricardo and his brothers miss

e. Jon remembered

52 **M1-4** | Verbs followed by gerunds or infinitives

Hacker/Sommers, *Exercises for A Canadian Writer's Reference,*
7th ed. (Boston: Bedford, 2019)

Exercise M2-1 ◆ Articles and types of nouns

Before working this exercise, read section M2 in *A Canadian Writer's Reference*, Seventh Edition.

Edit the following sentences for proper use of articles and nouns. If a sentence is correct, write "correct" after it. Answers appear in the answer key. Example:

~~The~~ Josefina's dance routine was flawless.

a.   Doing volunteer work often brings a satisfaction.

b.   As I looked out the window of the plane, I could see the Lions Bay.

c.   Melina likes to drink her coffees with lots of cream.

d.   Recovering from abdominal surgery requires patience.

e.   I completed the my homework assignment quickly.

Hacker/Sommers, *Exercises for A Canadian Writer's Reference,*
7th ed. (Boston: Bedford, 2019)

M2-1 | Articles and types of nouns   **53**

Exercise M2-2 ◆ Articles

Before working this exercise, read section M2 in *A Canadian Writer's Reference*, Seventh Edition.

Articles have been omitted from the following description of winter weather. Insert the articles *a, an,* and *the* where English requires them and be prepared to explain the reasons for your choices. Answers appear in the answer key.

Many people confuse terms *hail*, *sleet*, and *freezing rain*. Hail normally occurs in thunderstorm and is caused by strong updrafts that lift growing chunks of ice into clouds. When chunks of ice, called hailstones, become too heavy to be carried by updrafts, they fall to ground. Hailstones can cause damage to crops, windshields, and people. Sleet occurs during winter storms and is caused by snowflakes falling from layer of cold air into warm layer, where they become raindrops, and then into another cold layer. As they fall through last layer of cold air, raindrops freeze and become small ice pellets, forming sleet. When it hits car windshield or windows of house, sleet can make annoying racket. Driving and walking can be hazardous when sleet accumulates on roads and sidewalks. Freezing rain is basically rain that falls onto ground and then freezes after it hits ground. It causes icy glaze on trees and any surface that is below freezing.

Hacker/Sommers, *Exercises for A Canadian Writer's Reference,*
7th ed. (Boston: Bedford, 2019)

Exercise M3-1 ◆ Omissions and repetitions

Before working this exercise, read sections M3-a to M3-d in *A Canadian Writer's Reference*, Seventh Edition.

In the following sentences, add needed subjects or expletives (placeholders) and delete any repeated subjects, objects, or adverbs. Answers appear in the answer key. Example:

> **The new geology professor is the one whom we saw ~~him~~ on TV.**

a.   Are some cartons of ice cream in the freezer.

b.   I don't use the subway because am afraid.

c.   The prime minister she is the most popular leader in my country.

d.   We tried to get in touch with the same manager whom we spoke to him earlier.

e.   Recently have been a number of earthquakes in Turkey.

Exercise M3-2 ◆ Sentence structure

Before working this exercise, read sections M3-e and M3-f in *A Canadian Writer's Reference*, Seventh Edition.

Edit the following sentences for proper sentence structure. If a sentence is correct, write "correct" after it. Possible revisions appear in the answer key. Example:

She peeled ~~slowly~~ the banana/^{slowly.}

a.   Although freshwater freezes at 0 degrees Celsius, however ocean water freezes at –2 degrees Celsius.

b.   Because we switched cable packages, so our channel lineup has changed.

c.   The competitor mounted confidently his skateboard.

d.   My sister performs well the *legong*, a Balinese dance.

e.   Because product development is behind schedule, we will have to launch the product next spring.

Hacker/Sommers, *Exercises for A Canadian Writer's Reference,*
7th ed. (Boston: Bedford, 2019)

Exercise M4-1 ◆ Present versus past participles

Before working this exercise, read section M4-a in *A Canadian Writer's Reference*, Seventh Edition.

Edit the following sentences for proper use of present and past participles. If a sentence is correct, write "correct" after it. Answers appear in the answer key. Example:

> Danielle and Monica were very ~~exciting~~ *excited* to be going to a Broadway show for the first time.

a.   Listening to everyone's complaints all day was irritated.

b.   The long flight to Singapore was exhausted.

c.   His skill at chess is amazing.

d.   After a great deal of research, the scientist made a fascinated discovery.

e.   Surviving that tornado was one of the most frightened experiences I've ever had.

Hacker/Sommers, *Exercises for A Canadian Writer's Reference*, 7th ed. (Boston: Bedford, 2019)

M4-1 | Present versus past participles **57**

Exercise M4-2 ◆ Order of cumulative adjectives

Before working this exercise, read section M4-b in *A Canadian Writer's Reference*, Seventh Edition.

Arrange the following modifiers and nouns in their proper order. Answers appear in the answer key. Example:

> *two new French racing bicycles*
> **new, French, two, bicycles, racing**

a.   sculptor, young, an, Vietnamese, intelligent

b.   dedicated, a, priest, Catholic

c.   leather, worn, her, backpack, brown

d.   delicious, Joe's, Scandinavian, bread

e.   many, boxes, jewellery, antique, beautiful

Hacker/Sommers, *Exercises for A Canadian Writer's Reference*,
7th ed. (Boston: Bedford, 2019)

Exercise M5-1 ◆ Prepositions showing time and place

Before working this exercise, read section M5-a in *A Canadian Writer's Reference*, Seventh Edition.

In the following sentences, replace prepositions that are not used correctly. If a sentence is correct, write "correct" after it. Answers appear in the answer key. Example:

> *at*
> The play begins ~~on~~ 7:20 p.m.
> ^

a. Whenever we eat at the Centreville Café, we sit at a small table on the corner of the room.

b. In the 1990s, entrepreneurs created new online businesses in record numbers.

c. In Thursday, Nancy will attend her first home repair class at the community centre.

d. Alex began looking for her lost mitten in another location.

e. We decided to go to a restaurant because there was no fresh food on the refrigerator.

Hacker/Sommers, *Exercises for A Canadian Writer's Reference,*
7th ed. (Boston: Bedford, 2019)

M5-1 | Prepositions showing time and place   **59**

Exercise P1-1 ◆ The comma: Independent clauses, introductory elements

Before working this exercise, read sections P1-a and P1-b in *A Canadian Writer's Reference*, Seventh Edition.

Add or delete commas where necessary in the following sentences. If a sentence is correct, write "correct" after it. Answers appear in the answer key. Example:

> **Because we had been saving moulding for a few weeks, we had enough wood**
> **   ^**
> **to frame all thirty paintings.**

a.   Alisa brought the injured bird home, and fashioned a splint out of Popsicle sticks for its wing.

b.   Considered a classic of early animation *The Adventures of Prince Achmed* used hand-cut silhouettes against coloured backgrounds.

c.   If you complete the evaluation form and return it within two weeks you will receive a free breakfast during your next stay.

d.   After retiring from ballet in 1997, award-winning dancer Karen Kain went on to become the artistic director of the National Ballet of Canada.

e.   Roger had always wanted a handmade violin but he couldn't afford one.

60   P1-1 | The comma: Independent clauses, introductory elements

Hacker/Sommers, *Exercises for A Canadian Writer's Reference,*
7th ed. (Boston: Bedford, 2019)

Exercise P1-2 ◆ The comma: Independent clauses, introductory elements

Before working this exercise, read sections P1-a and P1-b in *A Canadian Writer's Reference*, Seventh Edition.

Add or delete commas where necessary in the following sentences. If a sentence is correct, write "correct" after it. Answers appear in the answer key. Example:

> **The car had been sitting idle for a month, so the battery was completely dead.**
> ^

a.   J. R. R. Tolkien finished writing his draft of the *Lord of the Rings* trilogy in 1949 but the first book in the series wasn't published until 1954.

b.   In the first two minutes of its ascent the space shuttle had broken the sound barrier and reached a height of over forty kilometres.

c.   German shepherds can be gentle guide dogs or they can be fierce attack dogs.

d.   Some former professional cyclists admit that the use of performance-enhancing drugs is widespread in cycling but they argue that no rider can be competitive without doping.

e.   As an intern, I learned most aspects of the broadcasting industry but I never learned about fundraising.

Exercise P1-3 ◆ The comma: Series, coordinate adjectives

Before working this exercise, read sections P1-c and P1-d in *A Canadian Writer's Reference*, Seventh Edition.

Add or delete commas where necessary in the following sentences. If a sentence is correct, write "correct" after it. Answers appear in the answer key. Example:

> **We gathered our essentials, took off for the great outdoors, and ignored the fact that it was Friday the 13th.**

a.   The cold impersonal atmosphere of the university was unbearable.

b.   An ambulance threaded its way through police cars, fire trucks and irate citizens.

c.   The *1812 Overture* is a stirring, magnificent piece of music.

d.   After two broken arms, three cracked ribs and one concussion, Ken quit the varsity football team.

e.   My cat's pupils had constricted to small black shining slits.

62   P1-3 | The comma: Series, coordinate adjectives

Hacker/Sommers, *Exercises for A Canadian Writer's Reference,*
7th ed. (Boston: Bedford, 2019)

Exercise P1-4 ◆ The comma: Series, coordinate adjectives

Before working this exercise, read sections P1-c and P1-d in *A Canadian Writer's Reference*, Seventh Edition.

Add or delete commas where necessary in the following sentences. If a sentence is correct, write "correct" after it. Answers appear in the answer key. Example:

> **Good social workers excel in patience, diplomacy‚ and positive thinking.**
>   ^

a. NASA's rovers on Mars are equipped with special cameras that can take close-up high-resolution pictures of the terrain.

b. A baseball player achieves the triple crown by having the highest batting average, the most home runs, and the most runs batted in during the regular season.

c. If it does not get enough sunlight, a healthy green lawn can turn into a shrivelled brown mess within a matter of days.

d. Love, vengeance, greed and betrayal are common themes in Western literature.

e. Many experts believe that shark attacks on surfers are a result of the sharks' mistaking surfboards for small, injured seals.

Hacker/Sommers, *Exercises for A Canadian Writer's Reference*,
7th ed. (Boston: Bedford, 2019)

P1-4 | The comma: Series, coordinate adjectives **63**

Exercise P1-5 ◆ The comma: Nonrestrictive elements

Before working this exercise, read section P1-e in *A Canadian Writer's Reference*, Seventh Edition.

Add or delete commas where necessary in the following sentences. If a sentence is correct, write "correct" after it. Answers appear in the answer key. Example:

> **My sister, who plays centre on the Sparks, now lives at Otter Point,**
> **a beach house near Sooke.**

a. Choreographer Louise Bédard's best-known work *Enfin vous zestes* is more than just a crowd-pleaser.

b. Marie Chouinard's contemporary ballet *24 Preludes by Chopin* is being performed by the National Ballet of Canada. [*Chouinard has written more than one contemporary ballet.*]

c. The glass sculptor sifting through hot red sand explained her technique to the other glassmakers. [*There is more than one glass sculptor.*]

d. A member of an organization, that provides job training for teens, was also appointed to the education commission.

e. Brian Eno who began his career as a rock musician turned to meditative compositions in the late 1970s.

Hacker/Sommers, *Exercises for A Canadian Writer's Reference,*
7th ed. (Boston: Bedford, 2019)

Exercise P1-6 ◆ The major uses of the comma

Before working this exercise, read sections P1-a to P1-e in *A Canadian Writer's Reference*, Seventh Edition.

This exercise covers the major uses of the comma described in P1-a to P1-e. Add or delete commas where necessary. If a sentence is correct, write "correct" after it. Answers appear in the answer key. Example:

> **Even though our brains actually can't focus on two tasks at a time‸ many people**
>
> **believe they can multitask.**

a. Cricket which originated in England is also popular in Australia, South Africa and India.

b. At the sound of the starting pistol the horses surged forward toward the first obstacle, a sharp incline one metre high.

c. After seeing an exhibition of Western art Gerhard Richter escaped from East Berlin, and smuggled out many of his notebooks.

d. Corrie's new wet suit has an intricate, blue pattern.

e. We replaced the rickety, old, spiral staircase with a sturdy, new ladder.

Exercise P1-7 ◆ The major uses of the comma

Before working this exercise, read sections P1-a to P1-f in *A Canadian Writer's Reference*, Seventh Edition.

This exercise covers the major uses of the comma described in P1-a to P1-f. Edit the following paragraph to correct any comma errors. Answers appear in the answer key.

Hope for Paws, a nonprofit rescue organization in Los Angeles tells many sad stories of animal abuse and neglect. Most of the stories, however have happy endings. One such story involves Woody, a dog left behind, after his master died. For a long lonely year, Woody took refuge under a neighbour's shed, waiting in vain, for his master's return. He survived on occasional scraps from his neighbours who eventually contacted Hope for Paws. When rescuers reached Woody, they found a malnourished, and frightened dog who had one blind eye and dirty, matted, fur. Gently, Woody was pulled from beneath the shed, and taken to the home of a volunteer, who fosters orphaned pets. There, Woody was fed, shaved, bathed and loved. Woody's story had the happiest of endings, when a family adopted him. Now Woody has a new forever home and he is once again a happy, well-loved dog.

Hacker/Sommers, *Exercises for A Canadian Writer's Reference*, 7th ed. (Boston: Bedford, 2019)

Exercise P1-8 ◆ All uses of the comma

Before working this exercise, read section P1 in *A Canadian Writer's Reference*, Seventh Edition.

This exercise covers all uses of the comma. Add or delete commas where necessary in the following sentences. If a sentence is correct, write "correct" after it. Answers appear in the answer key. Example:

> **"Yes, dear, you can have dessert," my mother said.**
> **^**

a.   On January 15, 2012 our office moved to 29 Commonwealth Avenue, Toronto ON M1K 4J8.

b.   The coach having resigned after the big game, we left the locker room in shock.

c.   Ms. Carlson you are a valued customer whose satisfaction is very important to us.

d.   Mr. Mundy was born on July 22, 1939 in Alberta, where his family had lived for four generations.

e.   Her board poised at the edge of the half-pipe, Nina waited her turn to drop in.

Exercise P2-1 ◆ Unnecessary commas

Before working this exercise, read section P2 in *A Canadian Writer's Reference*, Seventh Edition.

Delete any unnecessary commas in the following sentences. If a sentence is correct, write "correct" after it. Answers appear in the answer key. Example:

> **In his Silk Road Project, Yo-Yo Ma incorporates work by musicians such as/ Kayhan Kahlor and Richard Danielpour.**

a.   After the morning rains cease, the swimmers emerge from their cottages.

b.   Tricia's first artwork was a bright, blue, clay dolphin.

c.   Some modern musicians, (the group Beyond the Pale is an example) blend several cultural traditions into a unique sound.

d.   Myra liked hot, spicy foods such as, chili, kung pao chicken, and buffalo wings.

e.   On the display screen, was a soothing pattern of light and shadow.

Hacker/Sommers, *Exercises for A Canadian Writer's Reference,*
7th ed. (Boston: Bedford, 2019)

Exercise P2-2 ◆ Unnecessary commas

Before working this exercise, read section P2 in *A Canadian Writer's Reference*, Seventh Edition.

Delete unnecessary commas in the following passage. Answers appear in the answer key.

Each summer since 1980, Montreal has hosted the Montreal International Jazz Festival, an event that celebrates jazz music and musicians. Although, it is often referred to as "the Jazz Festival," it typically includes a wide variety of musical styles such as, electronica, Latin, big band, classical, and, rock and roll. Famous musicians who have appeared regularly at the Jazz Festival, include Oscar Peterson, B. B. King, and Aretha Franklin. Every year more than 650 concerts are held, which are seen by, close to 2.5 million visitors. Ten outdoor stages are located throughout the festival, and offer 450 free concerts. In 2015, the Jazz Festival marked its thirty-fifth anniversary. Fans, who could not attend the festival, still enjoyed the music by downloading MP3 files, and watching performances online.

Exercise P3-1 ◆ The semicolon and the colon

Before working this exercise, read sections P3-a to P3-c and review sections P1 and P2 in *A Canadian Writer's Reference*, Seventh Edition.

Add commas or semicolons where needed in the following well-known quotations. If a sentence is correct, write "correct" after it. Answers appear in the answer key. Example:

> If an animal does something, we call it instinct; if we do the same thing, we call it
>
> intelligence.   **—Will Cuppy**

a.   Do not ask me to be kind just ask me to act as though I were.   —Jules Renard

b.   If I ever have a conflict between art and nature I let art win.   —Robert Bateman

c.   When I get a little money I buy books if any is left I buy food and clothes.

                                                                   —Desiderius Erasmus

d.   The basis of my approach as a teacher has always been that we participate in

      society by means of our imagination or the quality of our social vision.   —Northrop Frye

e.   I detest life insurance agents they always argue that I shall

      some day die.   —Stephen Leacock

Exercise P3-2 ◆ The semicolon and the colon

Before working this exercise, read sections P3-a to P3-c and review sections P1 and P2 in *A Canadian Writer's Reference*, Seventh Edition.

Edit the following sentences to correct errors in the use of the comma and the semicolon. If a sentence is correct, write "correct" after it. Answers appear in the answer key. Example:

> **Love is blind; envy has its eyes wide open.**
>   ^

a.   Strong black coffee will not sober you up, the truth is that time is the only way to get alcohol out of your system.

b.   Margaret was not surprised to see hail and vivid lightning, conditions had been right for violent weather all day.

c.   There is often a fine line between right and wrong; good and bad; truth and deception.

d.   My mother always says that you can't learn common sense; either you're born with it or you're not.

e.   Severe, unremitting pain is a ravaging force; especially when the patient tries to hide it from others.

Hacker/Sommers, *Exercises for A Canadian Writer's Reference,*
7th ed. (Boston: Bedford, 2019)

P3-2 | The semicolon and the colon   **71**

Exercise P3-3 ◆ The comma, the semicolon, and the colon

Before working this exercise, read sections P3-d to P3-f and review sections P1 and P3-a to P3-c in *A Canadian Writer's Reference*, Seventh Edition.

Edit the following sentences to correct errors in the use of the comma, the semicolon, or the colon. If a sentence is correct, write "correct" after it. Answers appear in the answer key. Example:

> **Lifting the cover gently, Luca found the source of the odd soundː a marble in the**
>
> **gears.**

a.   We always looked forward to Thanksgiving in Winnipeg: It was our only chance to see our Grady cousins.

b.   If we have come to fight, we are far too few, if we have come to die, we are far too many.

c.   The travel package includes: a round-trip ticket to Athens, a cruise through the Cyclades, and all hotel accommodations.

d.   The news article portrays the land use proposal as reckless; although 62 percent of the town's residents support it.

e.   Psychologists Kindlon and Thompson (2000) offer parents a simple starting point for raising male children, "Teach boys that there are many ways to be a man" (p. 256).

Hacker/Sommers, *Exercises for A Canadian Writer's Reference,*
7th ed. (Boston: Bedford, 2019)

Exercise P4-1 ◆ The apostrophe

Before working this exercise, read section P4 in *A Canadian Writer's Reference*, Seventh Edition.

Edit the following sentences to correct errors in the use of the apostrophe. If a sentence is correct, write "correct" after it. Answers appear in the answer key. Example:

Richard's
Our favourite barbecue restaurant is Poor ~~Richards~~ Ribs.
^

a.   This diet will improve almost anyone's health.

b.   The innovative shoe fastener was inspired by the designers young son.

c.   Each days menu features a different European country's dish.

d.   Sue worked overtime to increase her families earnings.

e.   Ms. Jacobs is unwilling to listen to students complaints about computer failures.

Exercise P4-2 ◆ The apostrophe

Before working this exercise, read section P4 in *A Canadian Writer's Reference*, Seventh Edition.

Edit the following passage to correct errors in the use of the apostrophe. Answers appear in the answer key.

Its never too soon to start holiday shopping. In fact, some people choose to start shopping as early as January, when last seasons leftover's are priced at their lowest. Many stores try to lure customers in with promise's of savings up to 90 percent. Their main objective, of course, is to make way for next years inventory. The big problem with postholiday shopping, though, is that there isn't much left to choose from. Store's shelves have been picked over by last-minute shoppers desperately searching for gifts. The other problem is that its hard to know what to buy so far in advance. Next year's hot items are anyones guess. But proper timing, mixed with lot's of luck and determination, can lead to good purchases at great price's.

Hacker/Sommers, *Exercises for A Canadian Writer's Reference,*
7th ed. (Boston: Bedford, 2019)

Exercise P5-1 ◆ Quotation marks

Before working this exercise, read section P5 in *A Canadian Writer's Reference*, Seventh Edition.

Add or delete quotation marks as needed and make any other necessary changes in punctuation in the following sentences. If a sentence is correct, write "correct" after it. Answers appear in the answer key. Example:

> Gandhi once said, "An eye for an eye only ends up making the whole world blind."
>   ^   ^

a. As for the advertisement "Sailors have more fun", if you consider chipping paint and

    swabbing decks fun, then you will have plenty of it.

b. Even after forty minutes of discussion, our class could not agree on an interpretation of

    Robert Frost's poem "The Road Not Taken."

c. After winning the lottery, Juanita said that "she would give half the money to charity."

d. After the movie, Vicki said, "The reviewer called this flick "trash of the first order."

    I guess you can't believe everything you read."

e. "Cleaning your house while your kids are still growing," said Phyllis Diller, "is like

    shovelling the walk before it stops snowing."

Exercise P5-2 ◆ Quotation marks

Before working this exercise, read section P5 in *A Canadian Writer's Reference*, Seventh Edition.

Add or delete quotation marks as needed and make any other necessary changes in punctuation in the following passage. Citations should conform to MLA style (see MLA-4a). Answers appear in the answer key.

In his article The Moment of Truth, former US vice president Al Gore argues that global warming is a genuine threat to life on Earth and that we must act now to avoid catastrophe. Gore calls our situation a "true *planetary emergency*" and cites scientific evidence of the greenhouse effect and its consequences (170-71). "What is at stake, Gore insists, is the survival of our civilization and the habitability of the Earth (197)." With such a grim predicament at hand, Gore questions why so many political and economic leaders are reluctant to act. "Is it simply more convenient to ignore the warnings," he asks (171)?

The crisis, of course, will not go away if we just pretend it isn't there. Gore points out that in Chinese two symbols form the character for the word crisis. The first of those symbols means "danger", and the second means "opportunity." The danger we face, he claims, is accompanied by "unprecedented opportunity." (172) Gore contends that throughout history we have won battles against seemingly unbeatable evils such as slavery and fascism and that we did so by facing the truth and choosing the moral high ground. Gore's final appeal is to our humanity:

> "Ultimately, [the fight to end global warming] is not about any scientific discussion or political dialogue; it is about who we are as human beings. It is about our capacity to transcend our limitations, to rise to this new occasion. To see with our hearts, as well as our heads, the response that is now called for." (244)

Gore feels that the fate of our world rests in our own hands, and his hope is that we will make the choice to save the planet.

Source of quotations: Al Gore, "The Moment of Truth," *Vanity Fair*, May 2006, pp. 170+.

Exercise P6-1 ◆ The period, the question mark, and the exclamation point

Before working this exercise, read section P6-a in *A Canadian Writer's Reference*, Seventh Edition.

Add appropriate end punctuation in the following paragraph. Answers appear in the answer key.

Although I am generally rational, I am superstitious I never walk under ladders or put shoes on the table If I spill the salt, I go into frenzied calisthenics picking up the grains and tossing them over my left shoulder As a result of these curious activities, I've always wondered whether knowing the roots of superstitions would quell my irrational responses Superstition has it, for example, that one should never place a hat on the bed This superstition arises from a time when head lice were common and placing a guest's hat on the bed stood a good chance of spreading lice through the host's bed Doesn't this make good sense And doesn't it stand to reason that, if I know that my guests don't have lice, I shouldn't care where their hats go Of course it does It is fair to ask, then, whether I have changed my ways and place hats on beds Are you kidding I wouldn't put a hat on a bed if my life depended on it

Exercise P6-2 ◆ Other punctuation marks

Before working this exercise, read sections P6-b to P6-d in *A Canadian Writer's Reference*, Seventh Edition.

Edit the following sentences to correct errors in punctuation, focusing especially on appropriate use of the dash, parentheses, brackets, the ellipsis mark, and the slash. If a sentence is correct, write "correct" after it. Answers appear in the answer key. Example:

> Social insects/ —bees, for example/ —are able to communicate complicated
> ^   ^
> messages to one another.

a. A client left his/her cell phone in our conference room after the meeting.

b. The films we made of Kilauea—on our trip to Hawaii Volcanoes National

Park—illustrate a typical spatter cone eruption.

c. Although he was confident in his course selections, Greg chose the pass/fail option for

Chemistry 101.

d. Of three engineering fields, chemical, mechanical, and materials, Keegan chose materials

engineering for its application to toy manufacturing.

e. The writer Chitra Divakaruni explained her work with other Indian American

immigrants: "Many women who came to Maitri [a women's support group in San

Francisco] needed to know simple things like opening a bank account or getting

citizenship. . . . Many women in Maitri spoke English, but their English was functional

rather than emotional. They needed someone who understands their problems and speaks

their language."

Hacker/Sommers, *Exercises for A Canadian Writer's Reference,*
7th ed. (Boston: Bedford, 2019)

Exercise P7-1 ◆ Spelling

Before working this exercise, read sections P7-a and P7-c in *A Canadian Writer's Reference*, Seventh Edition.

The following memo has been run through a spell checker. Proofread it carefully, editing the spelling and typographical errors that remain. Answers appear in the answer key.

November 2, 2017

To: Patricia Wise

From: Constance Mayhew

Subject: Express Tours annual report

Thank you for agreeing to draft the annual report for Express Tours. Before you begin you're work, let me outline the initial steps.

First, its essential for you to include brief profiles of top management. Early next week, I'll provide profiles for all manages accept Samuel Heath, who's biographical information is being revised. You should edit these profiles carefully and than format them according to the enclosed instructions. We may ask you to include other employee's profiles at some point.

Second, you should arrange to get complete financial information for fiscal year 2017 from our comptroller, Richard Chang. (Helen Boyes, to, can provide the necessary figures.) When you get this information, precede according tot he plans we discuss in yesterday's meeting. By the way, you will notice from the figures that the sale of our Charterhouse division did not significantly effect net profits.

Third, you should email first draft of the report by December 11. Of coarse, you should proofread you writing.

I am quiet pleased that you can take on this project. If I can answers questions, don't hesitate to call.

Exercise P7-2 ◆ The hyphen

Before working this exercise, read sections P7-d to P7-h in *A Canadian Writer's Reference*, Seventh Edition.

Edit the following sentences to correct errors in hyphenation. If a sentence is correct, write "correct" after it. Answers appear in the answer key. Example:

> **Émile Zola's first readers were scandalized by his slice-of-life novels.**
> **^ ^**

a.   Gold is the seventy-ninth element in the periodic table.

b.   The swiftly-moving tugboat pulled alongside the barge and directed it away from the oil spill in the harbour.

c.   The ice-encrusted fossil was a major find.

d.   Your dog is well-known in our neighbourhood.

e.   Road-blocks were set up along all the major highways leading out of the city.

Hacker/Sommers, *Exercises for A Canadian Writer's Reference,*
7th ed. (Boston: Bedford, 2019)

Exercise P8-1 ◆ Capital letters

Before working this exercise, read section P8 in *A Canadian Writer's Reference*, Seventh Edition.

Edit the following sentences to correct errors in capitalization. If a sentence is correct, write "correct" after it. Answers appear in the answer key. Example:

>   L   G   B   K   H   P
> On our trip to the West, we visited the lions gate bridge and the kicking horse pass.

a.   Assistant dean Shirin Ahmadi recommended offering more world language courses.

b.   We went to the Tarragon Theatre to see a production of *Mr. Shi and His Lover*.

c.   Kalindi has an ambitious semester, studying differential calculus, classical hebrew, brochure design, and greek literature.

d.   Lydia's Aunt and Uncle make modular houses as beautiful as modernist works of art.

e.   We amused ourselves on the long flight by discussing how Spring in Kyoto stacks up against Summer in London.

Exercise P9-1 ◆ Abbreviations

Before working this exercise, read sections P9-a to P9-g in *A Canadian Writer's Reference*, Seventh Edition.

Edit the following sentences to correct errors in the use of abbreviations. If a sentence is correct, write "correct" after it. Answers appear in the answer key. Example:

Christmas   *Tuesday.*

This year ~~Xmas~~ will fall on a ~~Tues.~~
             ^   ^

a.   Since its inception, the CBC has maintained a consistently high standard of radio and

       television broadcasting.

b.   Some combat soldiers are trained by govt. diplomats to be sensitive to issues of culture,

       history, and religion.

c.   Mahatma Gandhi has inspired many modern leaders, including Martin Luther King Jr.

d.   How many kg have you lost since you began running six kilometres a day?

e.   Denzil spent all night studying for his psych. exam.

Hacker/Sommers, *Exercises for A Canadian Writer's Reference,*
7th ed. (Boston: Bedford, 2019)

Exercise P9-2 ◆ Numbers

Before working this exercise, read sections P9-h and P9-i in *A Canadian Writer's Reference*, Seventh Edition.

Edit the following sentences to correct errors in the use of numbers. If a sentence is correct, write "correct" after it. Answers appear in the answer key. Example:

$3.06
By the end of the evening, Ashanti had only ~~three dollars and six cents~~ left.
                                           ^

a.   The carpenters located 3 maple timbers, 21 sheets of cherry, and 10 oblongs of polished ebony for the theatre set.

b.   The program's cost is well over one billion dollars.

c.   The score was tied at 5–5 when the momentum shifted and carried the Standards to a decisive 12–5 win.

d.   8 students in the class had been labelled "learning disabled."

e.   The Canadian National Vimy Memorial in France had eleven thousand two hundred and eight-five names inscribed on it when it was unveiled in 1936.

Exercise P10-1 ◆ Italics

Before working this exercise, read section P10 in *A Canadian Writer's Reference*, Seventh Edition.

Edit the following sentences to correct errors in the use of italics. If a sentence is correct, write "correct" after it. Answers appear in the answer key. Example:

> **We had a lively discussion about Gini Alhadeff's memoir *The Sun at Midday*.** *Correct*

a. Howard Hughes commissioned the Spruce Goose, a beautifully built but thoroughly impractical wooden aircraft.

b. The old man *screamed* his anger, *shouting* to all of us, "I will not leave my money to you worthless layabouts!"

c. I learned the Latin term ad infinitum from an old nursery rhyme about fleas: "Great fleas have little fleas upon their back to bite 'em, / Little fleas have lesser fleas and so on ad infinitum."

d. Cinema audiences once gasped at hearing the word *damn* in *Gone with the Wind*.

e. Neve Campbell's lifelong interest in ballet inspired her involvement in the film "The Company," which portrays a season with the Joffrey Ballet.

Hacker/Sommers, *Exercises for A Canadian Writer's Reference*, 7th ed. (Boston: Bedford, 2019)

Exercise B1-1 ◆ Parts of speech: Nouns

Before working this exercise, read section B1-a in *A Canadian Writer's Reference*, Seventh Edition.

Underline the nouns (and noun/adjectives) in the following sentences. Answers appear in the answer key. Example:

> The best <u>part</u> of <u>dinner</u> was the <u>chef's</u> newest <u>dessert.</u>

a. The stage was set for a confrontation of biblical proportions.

b. The courage of the mountain climber was an inspiration to the rescuers.

c. The need to arrive before the guest of honour motivated us to navigate the thick fog.

d. The defence attorney made a final appeal to the jury.

e. A national museum dedicated to women artists opened in 1987.

Exercise B1-2 ◆ Parts of speech: Pronouns

Before working this exercise, read section B1-b in *A Canadian Writer's Reference*, Seventh Edition.

Underline the pronouns (and pronoun/adjectives) in the following sentences. Answers appear in the answer key. Example:

> <u>We</u> were intrigued by the video <u>that</u> the fifth graders produced as <u>their</u> final project.

a.   The premier's loyalty was <u>his</u> most appealing trait.

b.   In the fall, the geese <u>that</u> fly south for the winter pass through <u>our</u> town in huge numbers.

c.   As Carl Sandburg once said, even <u>he</u> <u>himself</u> did not understand <u>some</u> of <u>his</u> poetry.

d.   <u>I</u> appealed <u>my</u> parking ticket, but <u>you</u> did not get <u>one.</u>

e.   Angela did not mind gossip as long as <u>no one</u> gossiped about <u>her.</u>

Hacker/Sommers, *Exercises for A Canadian Writer's Reference,*
7th ed. (Boston: Bedford, 2019)

Exercise B1-3 ◆ Parts of speech: Verbs

Before working this exercise, read section B1-c in *A Canadian Writer's Reference*, Seventh Edition.

Underline the verbs in the following sentences, including helping verbs and particles. If a verb is part of a contraction (such as *is* in *isn't* or *would* in *I'd*), underline only the letters that represent the verb. Answers appear in the answer key. Example:

The ground under the pine trees <u>wasn't</u> wet from the rain.

a.   My grandmother always told me a soothing story before bed.

b.   There were fifty apples on the tree before the frost killed them.

c.   Morton brought down the box of letters from the attic.

d.   Stay on the main road and you'll arrive at the base camp before us.

e.   The fish struggled vigorously but was trapped in the net.

Exercise B1-4 ◆ Parts of speech: Adjectives and adverbs

Before working this exercise, read sections B1-d and B1-e in *A Canadian Writer's Reference*, Seventh Edition.

Underline the adjectives and circle the adverbs in the following sentences. If a word is a noun or pronoun functioning as an adjective, underline it and mark it as a noun/adjective or pronoun/adjective. Also treat the articles *a*, *an*, and *the* as adjectives. Answers appear in the answer key. Example:

> Finding <u>an</u> <u>available</u> room during <u>the</u> convention was (not) <u>easy</u>.

a.   Generalizations lead to weak, unfocused essays.

b.   The Spanish language is wonderfully flexible.

c.   The wildflowers smelled especially fragrant after the steady rain.

d.   I'd rather be slightly hot than bitterly cold.

e.   The cat slept soundly in its wicker basket.

Hacker/Sommers, *Exercises for A Canadian Writer's Reference*, 7th ed. (Boston: Bedford, 2019)

Exercise B2-1 ◆ Parts of sentences: Subjects

Before working this exercise, read section B2-a in *A Canadian Writer's Reference*, Seventh Edition.

In the following sentences, underline the complete subject and write *SS* above the simple subject(s). If the subject is an understood *you*, insert *you* in parentheses. Answers appear in the answer key. Example:

⌐SS⌐   ⌐SS⌐
Parents and their children often look alike.

a. The hills and mountains seemed endless, and the snow atop them glistened.

b. In foil fencing, points are scored by hitting an electronic target.

c. Do not stand in the aisles or sit on the stairs. *(you)*

d. There were hundreds of fireflies in the open field.

e. The evidence against the defendant was staggering.

(handwritten: word/group completes meaning of Subject by renaming / describing)

A **Exercise B2-2** ◆ **Parts of sentences: Subject complements and direct objects** → *(handwritten: word/group that names receiver of action)*

Before working this exercise, read section B2-b in *A Canadian Writer's Reference*, Seventh Edition.

Label the subject complements and direct objects in the following sentences, using the labels *SC* and *DO*. If a subject complement or a direct object consists of more than one word, bracket and label all of it. Answers appear in the answer key. Example:

$$\overline{\quad DO \quad}$$
The sharp right turn confused most drivers.

a. Mangoes are [expensive]. *(SC)*

b. Samurai warriors never fear [death]. *(DO)*

c. Successful coaches always praise [their players' efforts]. *(DO)*

★ d. St. Petersburg was [the capital of the Russian Empire] for two centuries. *(SC)*

e. The medicine tasted [bitter]. *(SC)*

Hacker/Sommers, *Exercises for A Canadian Writer's Reference,* 7th ed. (Boston: Bedford, 2019)

Exercise B2-3 ◆ Parts of sentences: Objects and complements

Before working this exercise, read section B2-b in *A Canadian Writer's Reference*, Seventh Edition.

Each of the following sentences has either an indirect object followed by a direct object or a direct object followed by an object complement. Label the objects and complements, using the labels *IO*, *DO*, and *OC*. If an object or a complement consists of more than one word, bracket and label all of it. Answers appear in the answer key. Example:

$$\overbrace{\hspace{3cm}}^{\text{DO}} \overbrace{\hspace{1.5cm}}^{\text{OC}}$$

Most people consider their own experience normal.

a.   Stress can make adults and children weary.

b.   The dining hall offered students healthy meal choices.

c.   Consider the work finished.

d.   We showed the agent our tickets, and she gave us boarding passes.

e.   Zita has made community service her priority this year.

[Handwritten notes:]

Indirect → noun/pronoun telling to or for whom action is done

Direct → noun/pronoun, word or group of words names receiver of action

Object Complement → word/group completes direct object's meaning by renaming/describing it.

Hacker/Sommers, *Exercises for A Canadian Writer's Reference*, 7th ed. (Boston: Bedford, 2019)

B2-3 | Parts of sentences: Objects and complements   **91**

Exercise B3-1 ◆ Subordinate word groups: Prepositional phrases

Before working this exercise, read section B3-a in *A Canadian Writer's Reference*, Seventh Edition.

Underline the prepositional phrases in the following sentences. Tell whether each one is an adjective phrase or an adverb phrase and what it modifies in the sentence. Answers appear in the answer key. Example:

> **Flecks <u>of mica</u> glittered <u>in the new granite floor</u>.** *(Adjective phrase modifying "Flecks"; adverb phrase modifying "glittered")*

a.   In northern Italy, we met many people who speak German as their first language.

b.   William completed the five-kilometre hike through the thick forest with ease.

c.   To my boss's dismay, I was late for work again.

d.   The travelling exhibit of Mayan artifacts gave viewers new insight into pre-Columbian culture.

e.   In 2002, the euro became the official currency in twelve European countries.

Hacker/Sommers, *Exercises for A Canadian Writer's Reference,*
7th ed. (Boston: Bedford, 2019)

Exercise B3-2 ◆ Subordinate word groups: Verbal phrases

Before working this exercise, read section B3-b in *A Canadian Writer's Reference*, Seventh Edition.

Underline the verbal phrases in the following sentences. Tell whether each phrase is participial, gerund, or infinitive and how each is used in the sentence. Answers appear in the answer key. Example:

Do you want <u>to watch that documentary</u>? *(Infinitive phrase used as direct object*

of "Do want")

a.   Updating your software will fix the computer glitch.

b.   The challenge in decreasing the town budget is identifying nonessential services.

c.   Cathleen tried to help her mother by raking the lawn.

d.   Understanding little, I had no hope of passing my biology final.

e.   Working with animals gave Steve a sense of satisfaction.

Exercise B3-3 ◆ Subordinate word groups: Subordinate clauses

Before working this exercise, read section B3-e in *A Canadian Writer's Reference*, Seventh Edition.

Underline the subordinate clauses in the following sentences. Tell whether each clause is an adjective clause, an adverb clause, or a noun clause and how it is used in the sentence. Answers appear in the answer key. Example:

> **Show the committee the latest draft <u>before you print the final report.</u>** *(Adverb clause modifying "Show")*

a.   The city's electoral commission adjusted the voting process so that every vote would count.

b.   A marketing campaign that targets baby boomers may not appeal to young professionals.

c.   After the Tambora volcano erupted in the southern Pacific in 1815, no one realized that it would contribute to the "year without a summer" in Europe and North America.

d.   The concept of peak oil implies that at a certain point there will be no more oil to extract from the earth.

e.   Details are easily overlooked when you are rushing.

Hacker/Sommers, *Exercises for A Canadian Writer's Reference,*
7th ed. (Boston: Bedford, 2019)

Exercise B4-1 ◆ Sentence types

Before working this exercise, read section B4 in *A Canadian Writer's Reference*, Seventh Edition.

Identify the following sentences as simple, compound, complex, or compound-complex. Identify the subordinate clauses and classify them according to their function: adjective, adverb, or noun. (See B3-e.) Answers appear in the answer key. Example:

> **The deli in Courthouse Square was crowded with lawyers at lunchtime.** *(Simple)*

a. Fires that are ignited in dry areas spread especially quickly.

b. The early Incas were advanced; they used a calendar and developed a decimal system.
Compound.

c. Elaine's jacket was too thin to block the wintry air.

d. Before we leave for the station, we always check the Via Rail website.
Complex

e. Decide when you want to leave, and I will be there to pick you up.

Subordinate clause → typically introduced by conjunction, forms part of + is dependent on main clause
ex. She answered the phone when it rang.
SC

Hacker/Sommers, *Exercises for A Canadian Writer's Reference,*
7th ed. (Boston: Bedford, 2019)

B4-1 | Sentence types **95**

Exercises for A Canadian Writer's Reference, Seventh Edition

Answer Key

Sentence Style

EXERCISE S1-1, page 1

Possible revisions:

a. Police dogs are used for finding lost children, tracking criminals, and detecting bombs and illegal drugs.
b. Hannah told her rock-climbing partner that she bought a new harness and that she wanted to climb Mount McConnell.
c. It is more difficult to sustain an exercise program than to start one.
d. During basic training, I was told not only what to do but also what to think.
e. Jan wanted to drive to the wine country or at least to the Niagara Escarpment.

EXERCISE S1-2, page 2

Possible revision:

Community service can provide tremendous benefits not only for the organization receiving the help but also for the volunteer providing the help. This dual benefit idea is behind a recent move to make community service hours a graduation requirement in high schools across the country. For many nonprofit organizations, seeking volunteers is often smarter financially than hiring additional employees. For many young people, community service positions can help develop empathy, commitment, and leadership. Opponents of the trend argue that volunteerism should not be mandatory, but research shows that community service requirements keep students engaged in school and lower dropout rates dramatically. Parents, school administrators, and community leaders all seem to favour the new initiatives.

EXERCISE S2-1, page 3

Possible revisions:

a. A grapefruit or an orange is a good source of vitamin C.
b. The women entering the military academy can expect haircuts as short as those of the male cadets.
c. Looking out the family room window, Sarah saw that her favourite tree, which she had climbed as a child, was gone.
d. The graphic designers are interested in and knowledgeable about producing posters for the balloon race.
e. The Great Barrier Reef is larger than any other coral reef in the world.

EXERCISE S3-1, page 4

Possible revisions:

a. More research is needed to evaluate effectively the risks posed by volcanoes in the Pacific Northwest.
b. Many students graduate from university with debt totalling more than twenty thousand dollars.
c. It is a myth that humans use only 10 percent of their brains.
d. A coolhunter is a person who can find the next wave of fashion in the unnoticed corners of modern society.
e. Not all geese fly beyond Kamloops for the winter.

EXERCISE S3-2, page 5

Possible revisions:

a. To complete an online purchase with a credit card, you must enter the expiration date and the security code.
b. Though Martha was only sixteen, UBC accepted her application.
c. As I settled in the cockpit, the pounding of the engine was muffled only slightly by my helmet.
d. After studying polymer chemistry, Phuong found computer games less complex.
e. When I was a young man, my mother enrolled me in tap dance classes.

EXERCISE S4-1, page 6

Possible revisions:

Version 1, first person

When online dating first became available, I thought that it would simplify romance. I believed that I could type in a list of criteria—sense of humour, postsecondary education, green eyes, good job—and a database would select the perfect mate for me. I signed up for some services and filled out my profile, confident that true love was only a few mouse clicks away. As it turns out, however, virtual dating is no easier than traditional dating. I still have to contact the people I find, exchange emails and phone calls, and meet them in the real world. Although a database might produce a list of possibilities and screen out obviously undesirable people, it can't predict chemistry. More often than not, I find that people who seem perfect online just don't click with me in person. Electronic services do help me expand my pool of potential dates, but they're no substitute for the hard work of romance.

Version 2, third person

When online dating first became available, many people thought that it would simplify romance. Hopeful singles believed that they could type in a list of criteria—sense of humour, postsecondary education, green eyes, good job—and a database would select the perfect mate. Thousands of people signed up for services and filled out their profiles, confident that true love was only a few mouse clicks away. As it turns out, however, virtual dating is no easier than traditional dating. Online daters still have to contact the people they find, exchange emails and phone calls, and meet in the real world. Although a database might produce a list of possibilities and screen out obviously undesirable people, it can't predict chemistry. More often than not, people who seem perfect online just don't click in person. Electronic services do help single people expand their pool of potential dates, but they're no substitute for the hard work of romance.

EXERCISE S4-2, page 7

Possible revision:

Settling Canada was arduous. Until 1608, many European attempts at permanent settlements—at Sable Island, Tadoussac, and Port Royal, for example—failed.

The first successful settlement began on July 3, 1608, when Samuel de Champlain founded Quebec for France.

Hacker/Sommers, *Exercises for A Canadian Writer's Reference*, 7th ed. (Boston: Bedford, 2019)

Answer Key **AK-1**

Although Champlain formed an alliance with the Algonquian and Montagnais peoples, survival was still difficult. To help his settlers develop skills, Champlain sent men to live with the Aboriginal peoples. These men were known as the *coureurs de bois* (runners of the woods).

Twenty-eight people originally settled Quebec. By 1630, the number had risen to only one hundred. The *coureurs de bois* extended the French influence to the Huron peoples in the Great Lakes area, but the English colonies were stronger. To bolster the French colony, in 1627 Cardinal Richelieu, regent of France, founded the Company of 100 Associates. He gave land to people to settle in New France and named Champlain governor.

Champlain was a prolific writer. He spent 1629 to 1632 writing a seven-hundred-page book called *Les voyages de la nouvelle France*. In his works, Champlain reveals nothing about himself; his meticulous descriptions of what he did and saw contain no value judgments and opinions. Thus, his works are the best account we have of the beginnings of Canadian history.

EXERCISE S4-3, page 8

Possible revisions:

a. A talented musician, Julie Crochetière uses R&B, soul, and jazz styles. She even performs pop music well.
b. Environmentalists point out that shrimp farming in Southeast Asia is polluting water and making farmlands useless. They warn that governments must act before it is too late.
c. We observed the samples for five days before we detected any growth. *Or* The samples were observed for five days before any growth was detected.
d. In his famous soliloquy, Hamlet contemplates whether death would be preferable to his difficult life and, if so, whether he is capable of committing suicide.
e. The lawyer told the judge that Miranda Hale was innocent and asked that she be allowed to prove the allegations false. *Or* The lawyer told the judge, "Miranda Hale is innocent. Please allow her to prove the allegations false."

EXERCISE S4-4, page 9

Possible revisions:

a. Courtroom lawyers need to have more than a touch of theatre in their blood.
b. The interviewer asked whether we had brought our proof of citizenship and our passports.
c. Experienced reconnaissance scouts know how to make fast decisions and use sophisticated equipment to keep their teams from being detected.
d. After the animators finish their scenes, the production designer arranges the clips according to the storyboard and makes synchronization notes for the sound editor and the composer.
e. Madame Defarge is a sinister figure in Dickens's *A Tale of Two Cities*. On a symbolic level, she represents fate; like the Greek Fates, she knits the fabric of individual destiny.

EXERCISE S5-1, page 10

Possible revisions:

a. Using surgical gloves is a precaution now taken by dentists to prevent contact with patients' blood and saliva.
b. A career in medicine, which my brother is pursuing, requires at least ten years of challenging work.
c. The pharaohs had bad teeth because tiny particles of sand found their way into Egyptian bread.
d. Recurring bouts of flu caused the team to forfeit a record number of games.
e. This box contains the key to your future.

EXERCISE S6-1, page 11

Possible revisions:

a. In 1987, Jenkins was elected to the Canadian Baseball Hall of Fame, and he was the first Canadian elected to the Baseball Hall of Fame in Cooperstown, New York.
b. Jenkins was the first Canadian pitcher to win the Cy Young Award; he also won the Lou Marsh Trophy as Canada's outstanding athlete in 1974.
c. Although he was grateful to have won the Cy Young Award, Jenkins felt that he should have won more awards.
d. Jenkins loved being a baseball pitcher; for example, he told *Baseball Almanac* that he didn't consider pitching to be work.
e. In the last forty years, Jenkins is the only Major League pitcher with six straight twenty-win seasons; he will likely be the last pitcher to do it because today's pitchers start fewer games.

EXERCISE S6-2, page 12

Possible revisions:

a. The X-Men comic books and Japanese woodcuts of kabuki dancers, all part of Marlena's research project on popular culture, covered the tabletop and the chairs.
b. Our waitress, costumed in a kimono, had painted her face white and arranged her hair in a lacquered beehive.
c. Students can apply for a spot in the leadership program, which teaches thinking and communication skills.
d. Shore houses were flooded up to the first floor, beaches were washed away, and Brant's Lighthouse was swallowed by the sea.
e. Laura Thackray, an engineer at Volvo Car Corporation, addressed women's safety needs by designing a pregnant crash-test dummy.

EXERCISE S6-3, page 13

Possible revisions:

a. These particles, known as "stealth liposomes," can hide in the body for a long time without detection.
b. Irena, a competitive gymnast majoring in biochemistry, intends to apply her athletic experience and her science degree to a career in sports medicine.
c. Because students, textile workers, and labour unions have loudly protested sweatshop abuses, apparel makers have been forced to examine their labour practices.
d. Developed in a European university, IRC (internet relay chat) was created as a way for a group of graduate students to talk about projects from their dorm rooms.
e. The cafeteria's new menu, which has an international flavour, includes everything from enchiladas and pizza to pad thai and sauerbraten.

EXERCISE S6-4, page 14

Possible revisions:

a. Working as an aide for the relief agency, Gina distributed food and medical supplies.
b. Janbir, who spent every Saturday learning tabla drumming, noticed with each hour of practice that his memory for complex patterns was growing stronger.
c. When the rotor hit, it gouged a hole about five millimetres deep in my helmet.
d. My grandfather, who was born eighty years ago in Puerto Rico, raised his daughters the old-fashioned way.
e. By reversing the depressive effect of the drug, the Narcan saved the patient's life.

Hacker/Sommers, *Exercises for A Canadian Writer's Reference,*
7th ed. (Boston: Bedford, 2019)

EXERCISE S7-1, page 15

Possible revisions:

a. Across the hall from the fossils exhibit are the exhibits for insects and spiders.
b. After growing up desperately poor in Japan, Sayuri becomes a successful geisha.
c. Researchers who have been studying Mount St. Helens for years believe that a series of earthquakes in the area may have caused the 1980 eruption.
d. Ice cream typically contains 10 percent milk fat, but premium ice cream may contain up to 16 percent milk fat and has considerably less air in the product.
e. If home values climb, the economy may recover more quickly than expected.

EXERCISE S7-2, page 16

Possible revision:

Making architectural models is a skill that requires patience and precision and is an art that illuminates a design. Architects come up with a grand and intricate vision, and then draftspersons convert that vision into blueprints. The model maker follows the blueprints to build a miniature version of the structure. Modellers can work in traditional materials like wood and clay and paint or in newer materials like Styrofoam and liquid polymers. Some modellers still use cardboard, paper, and glue; other modellers prefer glue guns, deformable plastic, and thin aluminum and brass wire. Although the modeller may seem to be making a small mess in the early stages of model building, in the end the modeller has completed a small-scale structure. Architect Rem Koolhaas has insisted that plans reveal the logic of a design and that models expose the architect's vision. The model maker's art makes this vision real.

Word Choice

EXERCISE W2-1, page 17

Possible revisions:

a. Martin Luther King Jr. set a high standard for future leaders.
b. Alice has loved cooking since she could first peek over a kitchen tabletop.
c. Bloom's race to be premier is futile.
d. A successful graphic designer must have technical knowledge and an eye for colour and balance.
e. You will deliver mail to all employees.

EXERCISE W2-2, page 18

Possible revision:

To: District managers
From: Margaret Davenport, Vice President
Subject: Customer database

Some of our sales representatives have been failing to log daily reports of their client calls in our customer database. Also, some representatives are not routinely checking the database. Our clients sometimes receive repeated sales calls from us when a sales representative does not realize that the client has already been contacted. Repeated calls annoy our customers and make us appear disorganized.

Effective immediately, direct your representatives to do the following:

• Record each customer contact in the customer database at the end of each day.
• Check the database at the beginning of each day to avoid repeated calls.

Thank you for your cooperation in this important matter.

EXERCISE W3-1, page 19

Possible revisions:

a. The Prussians defeated the Saxons in 1745.
b. Ahmed, the producer, manages the entire operation.
c. The tour guides expertly paddled the sea kayaks.
d. Emphatic and active; no change
e. Protesters were shouting on the courthouse steps.

EXERCISE W3-2, page 20

a. passive; b. active; c. passive; d. active; e. active

EXERCISE W4-1, page 21

Possible revisions:

a. When I was young, my family was poor.
b. This conference will help me serve my clients better.
c. The meteorologist warned the public about the possible dangers of the coming storm.
d. Government studies show a need for after-school programs.
e. Passengers should try to complete the customs declaration form before leaving the plane.

EXERCISE W4-2, page 22

Possible revision:

Dear Ms. Jackson:

We at Nakamura Reyes value our relationship with Creative Software, and I look forward to seeing you next week at the trade show in Fresno. Please let me know when you will have time to meet with Mr. Reyes and me to discuss our production schedule. It's crucial that we all agree on our 2017–2018 product release dates.

Before we meet, however, I have some new information. Our user-friendly approach to the new products will make longer user testing periods necessary. The enclosed data should help you adjust your timeline; let me know right away if you require any additional information before making these adjustments.

Before we meet in Fresno, Mr. Reyes and I will outline any other topics for discussion. Thanks for your help.

Sincerely,
Sylvia Nakamura

EXERCISE W4-3, page 23

Possible revisions:

Version 1, for a general audience

In popular culture, college or university graduates who return home to live with their parents are seen as irresponsible freeloaders. And many older adults seem to feel that the trend of moving back home after school, which was rare in their day, is becoming too commonplace today. But society must realize that a cultural shift is taking place. Most young adults want to live on their own as soon as possible, but they graduate with large amounts of debt and need some time to become financially stable. College or university tuition and the cost of housing have increased far beyond the pace of salary increases in the past fifty years. Also, the job market is tighter and more jobs require advanced degrees than in the past. So before people criticize college or university graduates who temporarily move back into their parents' house, they must consider all the facts.

Version 2, for an audience of young adults

In popular culture, college or university grads who return home to live with their parents are seen as irresponsible slackers. And many older adults seem to feel that the trend of moving back home after school, which was rare in their day, is too common today. But society should understand

Hacker/Sommers, *Exercises for A Canadian Writer's Reference,*
7th ed. (Boston: Bedford, 2019)

Answer Key **AK-3**

that times have changed. Most young adults want to live on their own right away, but they graduate with tons of debt and need some time to get back on their feet financially. College or university tuition and the cost of housing have increased far beyond salary increases in the past fifty years. Also, the job market is tighter and more jobs require degrees than in the past. So before people criticize college or university grads who move back home for a while, they should be sure to consider all the facts.

EXERCISE W4-4, page 24

Possible revisions:

a. Dr. Geralyn Farmer is the chief surgeon at University Hospital. Dr. Paul Green is her assistant.
b. All applicants want to know how much they will earn.
c. Elementary school teachers should understand the concept of nurturing if they intend to be effective.
d. Obstetricians need to be available to their patients at all hours.
e. If we do not stop polluting our environment, we will perish.

NOTE: Since it is becoming increasingly acceptable to use the plural pronoun *they* to refer to an indefinite pronoun or a generic noun, sentences b, c, and d could have alternative revisions. For example, this sentence could be considered acceptable: *Every applicant wants to know how much they will earn.*

EXERCISE W4-5, page 25

Possible revision:

We are looking for qualified candidates for the position of elementary school teacher. The ideal candidate should have a bachelor's degree, a teaching certificate, and one year of student teaching. Candidates should be knowledgeable in all elementary subject areas. We want our new teacher to have a commanding presence in the classroom as well as a patient and trustworthy demeanor. The teacher must be able to both motivate an entire classroom and work with students one-on-one to assess their individual needs. The teacher must also be comfortable communicating with the students' parents. For salary and benefits information, please contact the Upper Canada District School Board. Qualified applicants should submit their résumés by March 15.

EXERCISE W5-2, page 27

Possible revisions:

a. We regret this delay; thank you for your patience.
b. Ada's plan is to acquire education and experience to prepare herself for a position as property manager.
c. Serena Williams, the ultimate competitor, has earned millions of dollars just in endorsements.
d. Many people take for granted that public libraries have up-to-date computer systems.
e. The effect of Gao Xingjian's novels on other Chinese exiles is hard to gauge.

EXERCISE W5-3, page 28

Possible revisions:

a. Queen Anne was so angry with Sarah Churchill that she refused to see her again.
b. Correct
c. The parade moved off the street and onto the beach.
d. The frightened refugees intend to make the dangerous trek across the mountains.
e. What type of wedding are you planning?

EXERCISE W5-4, page 29

Possible revisions:

a. John stormed into the room like a hurricane.
b. Some people insist that they'll always be available to help, even when they haven't been before.

c. The Blue Jays easily beat the Mets, who were in trouble early in the game today the Rogersentre.
d. We worked out the problems in our relationship.
e. My mother accused me of evading her questions when in fact I was just saying the first thing that came to mind.

Grammatical Sentences

EXERCISE G1-1, page 30

a. One of the main reasons for elephant poaching is the profits received from selling the ivory tusks.
b. Correct
c. A number of students in the seminar were aware of the importance of joining the discussion.
d. Batik cloth from Bali, blue and white ceramics from Delft, and a bocce ball from Turin have made Angelie's room the talk of the dorm.
e. Correct

EXERCISE G1-2, page 31

Subject: turtles; verb: migrate; Subject: season; verb: spans; Subject: habitat; verb: ranges; Subject: nesting; verb: takes; Subject: turtles; verb: crawl; Subject: cavity; verb: is; Subject: eggs; verb: are; Subject: eggs; verb: begin; Subject: cause; verb: is; Subject: erosion and development; verb: threaten; Subject: crowd or lights; verb: are

EXERCISE G2-1, page 32

a. When I get the urge to exercise, I lie down until it passes.
b. Grandmother had driven our new hybrid to the sunrise church service, so we were left with the station wagon.
c. A pile of dirty rags was lying at the bottom of the stairs.
d. How did the game know that the player had gone from the room with the blue ogre to the hall where the gold was heaped?
e. The computer programmer was an expert in online security; he was confident that the encryption code he used could never be broken.

EXERCISE G2-2, page 33

a. The glass sculptures of the Swan Boats were prominent in the brightly lit lobby.
b. Visitors to the glass museum were not supposed to touch the exhibits.
c. Our church has all the latest technology, even a closed-circuit television.
d. Christos didn't know about Marlo's promotion because he never listens. He is [or He's] always talking.
e. Correct

EXERCISE G2-3, page 34

a. Correct
b. Watson and Crick discovered the mechanism that controls inheritance in all life: the workings of the DNA molecule.
c. When city planners proposed rezoning the waterfront, did they know that the mayor had promised to curb development in that neighbourhood.
d. Tonight's concert begins at 9:30. If it were earlier, I'd consider going.
e. Correct

EXERCISE G3-1, page 35

Possible revisions:

a. Every candidate for prime minister must appeal to a wide variety of ethnic and social groups to win the election.

Hacker/Sommers, *Exercises for A Canadian Writer's Reference,* 7th ed. (Boston: Bedford, 2019)

b. Either Tom Hanks or Harrison Ford will win an award for his lifetime achievement in cinema.
c. The aerobics teacher motioned for all the students to move their arms in wide, slow circles.
d. Correct
e. Applicants should be bilingual if they want to qualify for this position.

NOTE: Since it is becoming increasingly acceptable to use the plural pronoun *they* to refer to an indefinite pronoun or a generic noun, sentences a, c, and e could be labeled correct as written.

EXERCISE G3-2, page 36

Possible revision:

A common practice in businesses is to put each employee in a cubicle. A typical cubicle resembles an office, but its walls don't reach the ceiling. Many office managers feel that a cubicle floor plan has its advantages. Cubicles make a large area feel spacious. In addition, they can be moved around so that new employees can be accommodated in their own work area. Of course, the cubicle model also has problems. Typically, employees are not as happy with a cubicle as they would be with a traditional office. Also, productivity can suffer. Neither a manager nor a frontline worker can ordinarily do his or her best work in a cubicle because of noise and lack of privacy. Workers can hear their neighbours tapping on keyboards, making phone calls, and muttering under their breath.

EXERCISE G3-3, page 37

Possible revisions:

a. Some professors say that engineering students should have hands-on experience with dismantling and reassembling machines.
b. Because she had decorated her living room with posters from chamber music festivals, her date thought that she was interested in classical music. Actually she preferred rock.
c. In my high school, students didn't need to get all A's to be considered a success; they just needed to work to their ability.
d. Marianne told Jenny, "I am worried about your mother's illness." [*or* ". . . about my mother's illness."]
e. Though Lewis cried for several minutes after scraping his knee, eventually his crying subsided.

EXERCISE G3-4, page 38

Possible revision:

Since its launch in the 1980s, the internet has grown to be one of the largest communications forums in the world. The internet was created by a team of academics who were building on a platform that government scientists had started developing in the 1950s. The creators initially viewed the internet as a noncommercial enterprise that would serve only the needs of the academic and technical communities. But with the introduction of user-friendly browser technology in the 1990s, personal and commercial internet use expanded tremendously. By the late 1990s, many businesses were connecting to the internet with high-speed broadband and fibre-optic connections, technology available to many home users today. Accessing information, shopping, gaming, and communicating are easier than ever before. These conveniences, however, can lead to some possible drawbacks. Computer users forfeit privacy when they search, shop, game, and communicate. Computer experts advise that avoiding disclosure of personal information and routinely adjusting privacy settings on social media sites are the best ways for users to protect themselves on the internet.

EXERCISE G3-5, page 39

a. Correct [But the writer could change the end of the sentence: . . . *than he was.*]
b. Correct [But the writer could change the end of the sentence: . . . *that she was the coach.*]
c. She appreciated his telling the truth in such a difficult situation.
d. The director has asked you and me to draft a proposal for a new recycling plan.
e. Five close friends and I rented a station wagon, packed it with food, and drove two hundred kilometres to the Calgary Stampede.

EXERCISES G3-6, page 40

her, he, she, them, their

EXERCISE G3-7, page 41

a. Correct
b. The environmental policy conference featured scholars whom I had never heard of. [*or* . . . scholars I had never heard of.]
c. Correct
d. Daniel always gives a holiday donation to whoever needs it.
e. So many singers came to the audition that Natalia had trouble deciding whom to select for the choir.

EXERCISE G4-1, page 42

Possible revisions:

a. Do you expect to perform well on the nursing board exam next week?
b. With the budget deadline approaching, our office has hardly had time to handle routine correspondence.
c. Correct
d. The customer complained that he hadn't been treated nicely by the agent on the phone.
e. Of all the smart people in my family, Uncle Roberto is the cleverest. [*or* . . . most clever.]

EXERCISE G4-2, page 43

Possible revision:

Doctors recommend that to give skin the fullest protection from ultraviolet rays, people should use plenty of sunscreen, limit sun exposure, and wear protective clothing. The most common sunscreens today are known as "broad spectrum" because they block out both UVA and UVB rays. These lotions don't feel any different on the skin from the old UVA-only types, but they work better at preventing premature aging and skin cancer.

Many sunscreens claim to be waterproof, but they won't provide adequate coverage after extended periods of swimming or perspiring. To protect well, even waterproof sunscreens should be reapplied liberally and often. All areas of exposed skin, including ears, backs of hands, and tops of feet, need to be coated well to avoid burning or damage. Some people's skin reacts badly to PABA, or para-aminobenzoic acid, so PABA-free (hypoallergenic) sunscreens are widely available. In addition to recommending sunscreen, most doctors agree that people should stay out of the sun when rays are the strongest—between 10:00 a.m. and 3:00 p.m.—and should limit time in the sun. They also suggest that people wear long-sleeved shirts, broad-brimmed hats, and long pants whenever possible.

EXERCISE G5-1, page 44

Possible revisions:

a. Listening to the CD her sister had sent, Mia was overcome with a mix of emotions: happiness, homesickness, and nostalgia.

b. Cortés and his soldiers were astonished when they looked down from the mountains and saw Tenochtitlán, the magnificent capital of the Aztecs.

c. Although my spoken French is not very good, I can read the language with ease.

d. There are several reasons for not eating meat. One reason is that dangerous chemicals are used throughout the various stages of meat production.

e. To learn how to sculpt beauty from everyday life is my intention in studying art and archaeology.

EXERCISE G5-2, page 45

Possible revision:

Digital technology has revolutionized information delivery, forever blurring the lines between information and entertainment. Yesterday's readers of books and newspapers are today's readers of e-books and blogs. Countless readers have moved on from print information entirely, choosing instead to point, click, and scroll their way through a text online or on an e-reader. Once a nation of people spoon-fed television commercials and the six o'clock evening news, we are now seemingly addicted to YouTube and social media. Remember the family trip when Dad or Mom wrestled with a road map on the way to Banff or Whistler? No wrestling is required with a GPS device—unless it's Mom and Dad wrestling over who gets to program the address. Accessing information now seems to be Canada's favourite pastime. Statistics Canada, in its Canadian Internet Use Survey, reports that 80 percent of Canadian adults use the internet for personal reasons, connecting mostly from home. As a country, we embrace information and communication technologies, which now include smartphones and tablets. Among children and adolescents, social media and other technology use are well established for activities like socializing, gaming, and information gathering.

EXERCISE G6-1, page 46

Possible revisions:

a. The city had one public swimming pool that stayed packed with children all summer long.

b. The building is being renovated, so at times we have no heat, water, or electricity.

c. The view was not what the travel agent had described. Where were the rolling hills and the shimmering rivers?

d. Walker's coming-of-age novel is set against a gloomy scientific backdrop; the Earth's rotation has begun to slow down.

e. City officials had good reason to fear a major earthquake: Most [*or* most] of the business district was built on landfill.

EXERCISE G6-2, page 47

Possible revisions:

a. Wind power for the home is a supplementary source of energy that can be combined with electricity, gas, or solar energy.

b. Correct

c. In the Middle Ages, when the streets of London were dangerous places, it was safer to travel by boat along the Thames.

d. "He's not drunk," I said. "He's in insulin shock."

e. Are you able to endure extreme angle turns, high speeds, frequent jumps, and occasional crashes? Then supermoto racing may be a sport for you.

EXERCISE G6-3, page 48

Possible revision:

Some parents and educators argue that requiring uniforms in public schools would improve student behaviour and performance. They think that uniforms give students a more professional attitude toward school; moreover, they believe that uniforms help create a sense of community among students from diverse backgrounds. But parents and educators should consider the drawbacks to requiring uniforms in public schools.

Although uniforms do create a sense of community, they do this by stamping out individuality. Youth is a time to express originality, a time to develop a sense of self. One important way young people express their identities is through the clothes they wear. The self-patrolled dress code of high school students may be stricter than any school-imposed code. Nevertheless, trying to control dress habits from above will only lead to resentment or to mindless conformity.

If children are going to act like adults, they need to be treated like adults and to be allowed to make their own choices. Telling young people what to wear to school merely prolongs their childhood. Requiring uniforms undermines the educational purpose of public schools, which is not just to teach facts and figures but to help young people grow into adults who are responsible for making their own choices.

Multilingual Writers and ESL Topics

EXERCISE M1-1, page 49

a. In the past, tobacco companies denied any connection between smoking and health problems.

b. The volunteer's compassion has touched many lives.

c. I want to register for a summer tutoring session.

d. By the end of the year, the province will have tested 139 birds for avian flu.

e. The golfers were prepared for all weather conditions.

EXERCISE M1-2, page 50

a. A major league pitcher can throw a baseball more than ninety-five miles per hour.

b. The writing centre tutor will help you revise your essay.

c. A reptile must adjust its body temperature to its environment.

d. Correct

e. My uncle, a cartoonist, could sketch a face in less than a minute.

EXERCISE M1-3, page 51

Possible revisions:

a. The electrician might have discovered the broken circuit if she had gone through the modules one at a time.

b. If Verena wins a scholarship, she will go to graduate school.

c. Whenever a rainbow appears after a storm, everybody comes out to see it.

d. Sarah did not understand the terms of her internship.

e. If I lived in Budapest with my cousin Szusza, she would teach me Hungarian cooking.

EXERCISE M1-4, page 52

Possible answers:

a. I enjoy riding my motorcycle.

b. The tutor told Samantha to come to the writing centre.

c. The team hopes to work hard and win the championship.

d. Ricardo and his brothers miss surfing during the winter.

e. Jon remembered to lock the door. *Or* Jon remembered seeing that movie years ago.

Hacker/Sommers, *Exercises for A Canadian Writer's Reference,*
7th ed. (Boston: Bedford, 2019)

EXERCISE M2-1, page 53

a. Doing volunteer work often brings satisfaction.
b. As I looked out the window of the plane, I could see Lions Bay.
c. Melina likes to drink her coffee with lots of cream.
d. Correct
e. I completed my homework assignment quickly. *Or* I completed the homework assignment quickly.

EXERCISE M2-2, page 54

Many people confuse the terms *hail*, *sleet*, and *freezing rain*. Hail normally occurs in a thunderstorm and is caused by strong updrafts that lift growing chunks of ice into the clouds. When the chunks of ice, called hailstones, become too heavy to be carried by the updrafts, they fall to the ground. Hailstones can cause damage to crops, windshields, and people. Sleet occurs during winter storms and is caused by snowflakes falling from a layer of cold air into a warm layer, where they become raindrops, and then into another cold layer. As they fall through the last layer of cold air, the raindrops freeze and become small ice pellets, forming sleet. When it hits a car windshield or the windows of a house, sleet can make an annoying racket. Driving and walking can be hazardous when sleet accumulates on roads and sidewalks. Freezing rain is basically rain that falls onto the ground and then freezes after it hits the ground. It causes an icy glaze on trees and any surface that is below freezing.

EXERCISE M3-1, page 55

a. There are some cartons of ice cream in the freezer.
b. I don't use the subway because I am afraid.
c. The prime minister is the most popular leader in my country.
d. We tried to get in touch with the same manager whom we spoke to earlier.
e. Recently there have been a number of earthquakes in Turkey.

EXERCISE M3-2, page 56

Possible revisions:

a. Although freshwater freezes at 0 degrees Celsius, ocean water freezes at −2 degrees Celsius.
b. Because we switched cable packages, our channel lineup has changed.
c. The competitor confidently mounted his skateboard.
d. My sister performs the *legong*, a Balinese dance, well.
e. Correct

EXERCISE M4-1, page 57

a. Listening to everyone's complaints all day was irritating.
b. The long flight to Singapore was exhausting.
c. Correct
d. After a great deal of research, the scientist made a fascinating discovery.
e. Surviving that tornado was one of the most frightening experiences I've ever had.

EXERCISE M4-2, page 58

a. an intelligent young Vietnamese sculptor
b. a dedicated Catholic priest
c. her worn brown leather backpack
d. Joe's delicious Scandinavian bread
e. many beautiful antique jewellery boxes

EXERCISE M5-1, page 59

a. Whenever we eat at the Centreville Café, we sit at a small table in the corner of the room.
b. Correct
c. On Thursday, Nancy will attend her first home repair class at the community centre.
d. Correct
e. We decided to go to a restaurant because there was no fresh food in the refrigerator.

Punctuation and Mechanics

EXERCISE P1-1, page 60

a. Alisa brought the injured bird home and fashioned a splint out of Popsicle sticks for its wing.
b. Considered a classic of early animation, *The Adventures of Prince Achmed* used hand-cut silhouettes against coloured backgrounds.
c. If you complete the evaluation form and return it within two weeks, you will receive a free breakfast during your next stay.
d. Correct
e. Roger had always wanted a handmade violin, but he couldn't afford one.

EXERCISE P1-2, page 61

a. J. R. R. Tolkien finished writing his draft of the *Lord of the Rings* trilogy in 1949, but the first book in the series wasn't published until 1954.
b. In the first two minutes of its ascent, the space shuttle had broken the sound barrier and reached a height of over forty kilometres.
c. German shepherds can be gentle guide dogs, or they can be fierce attack dogs.
d. Some former professional cyclists admit that the use of performance-enhancing drugs is widespread in cycling, but they argue that no rider can be competitive without doping.
e. As an intern, I learned most aspects of the broadcasting industry, but I never learned about fundraising.

EXERCISE P1-3, page 62

a. The cold, impersonal atmosphere of the university was unbearable.
b. An ambulance threaded its way through police cars, fire trucks, and irate citizens.
c. Correct
d. After two broken arms, three cracked ribs, and one concussion, Ken quit the varsity football team.
e. Correct

EXERCISE P1-4, page 63

a. NASA's rovers on Mars are equipped with special cameras that can take close-up, high-resolution pictures of the terrain.
b. Correct
c. Correct
d. Love, vengeance, greed, and betrayal are common themes in Western literature.
e. Many experts believe that shark attacks on surfers are a result of the sharks' mistaking surfboards for small injured seals.

EXERCISE P1-5, page 64

a. Choreographer Louise Bédard's best-known work, *Enfin vous zestes*, is more than just a crowd-pleaser.
b. Correct
c. Correct

Hacker/Sommers, *Exercises for A Canadian Writer's Reference*, 7th ed. (Boston: Bedford, 2019)

Answer Key **AK-7**

d.   A member of an organization that provides job training for teens was also appointed to the education commission.

e.   Brian Eno, who began his career as a rock musician, turned to meditative compositions in the late 1970s.

EXERCISE P1-6, page 65

a.   Cricket, which originated in England, is also popular in Australia, South Africa, and India.

b.   At the sound of the starting pistol, the horses surged forward toward the first obstacle, a sharp incline one metre high.

c.   After seeing an exhibition of Western art, Gerhard Richter escaped from East Berlin and smuggled out many of his notebooks.

d.   Corrie's new wet suit has an intricate blue pattern.

e.   We replaced the rickety old spiral staircase with a sturdy new ladder.

EXERCISE P1-7, page 66

Hope for Paws, a nonprofit rescue organization in Los Angeles, tells many sad stories of animal abuse and neglect. Most of the stories, however, have happy endings. One such story involves Woody, a dog left behind after his master died. For a long, lonely year, Woody took refuge under a neighbour's shed, waiting in vain for his master's return. He survived on occasional scraps from his neighbours, who eventually contacted Hope for Paws. When rescuers reached Woody, they found a malnourished and frightened dog who had one blind eye and dirty, matted fur. Gently, Woody was pulled from beneath the shed and taken to the home of a volunteer who fosters orphaned pets. There, Woody was fed, shaved, bathed, and loved. Woody's story had the happiest of endings when a family adopted him. Now Woody has a new forever home, and he is once again a happy, well-loved dog.

EXERCISE P1-8, page 67

a.   On January 15, 2012, our office moved to 29 Commonwealth Avenue, Toronto, ON M1K 4J8.

b.   Correct

c.   Ms. Carlson, you are a valued customer whose satisfaction is very important to us.

d.   Mr. Mundy was born on July 22, 1939, in Alberta, where his family had lived for four generations.

e.   Correct

EXERCISE P2-1, page 68

a.   Correct

b.   Tricia's first artwork was a bright blue clay dolphin.

c.   Some modern musicians (the group Beyond the Pale is an example) blend several cultural traditions into a unique sound.

d.   Myra liked hot, spicy foods such as chili, kung pao chicken, and buffalo wings.

e.   On the display screen was a soothing pattern of light and shadow.

EXERCISE P2-2, page 69

Each summer since 1980, Montreal has hosted the Montreal International Jazz Festival, an event that celebrates jazz music and musicians. Although it is often referred to as "the Jazz Festival," it typically includes a wide variety of musical styles such as electronica, Latin, big band, classical, and rock and roll. Famous musicians who have appeared regularly at the Jazz Festival include Oscar Peterson, B. B. King, and Aretha Franklin. Every year more than 650 concerts are held, which are seen by close to 2.5 million visitors. Ten outdoor stages are located throughout the festival and offer 450 free concerts. In 2015, the Jazz Festival marked its thirty-fifth anniversary. Fans who could not attend the festival still enjoyed the music by downloading MP3 files and watching performances online.

EXERCISE P3-1, page 70

a.   Do not ask me to be kind; just ask me to act as though I were.

b.   If I ever have a conflict between art and nature, I let art win.

c.   When I get a little money, I buy books; if any is left, I buy food and clothes.

d.   Correct

e.   I detest life insurance agents; they always argue that I shall some day die.

EXERCISE P3-2, page 71

a.   Strong black coffee will not sober you up; the truth is that time is the only way to get alcohol out of your system.

b.   Margaret was not surprised to see hail and vivid lightning; conditions had been right for violent weather all day.

c.   There is often a fine line between right and wrong, good and bad, truth and deception.

d.   Correct

e.   Severe, unremitting pain is a ravaging force, especially when the patient tries to hide it from others.

EXERCISE P3-3, page 72

a.   Correct [Either *It* or *it* is correct.]

b.   If we have come to fight, we are far too few; if we have come to die, we are far too many.

c.   The travel package includes a round-trip ticket to Athens, a cruise through the Cyclades, and all hotel accommodations.

d.   The news article portrays the land use proposal as reckless, although 62 percent of the town's residents support it.

e.   Psychologists Kindlon and Thompson (2000) offer parents a simple starting point for raising male children: "Teach boys that there are many ways to be a man" (p. 256).

EXERCISE P4-1, page 73

a.   Correct

b.   The innovative shoe fastener was inspired by the designer's young son.

c.   Each day's menu features a different European country's dish.

d.   Sue worked overtime to increase her family's earnings.

e.   Ms. Jacobs is unwilling to listen to students' complaints about computer failures.

EXERCISE P4-2, page 74

It's never too soon to start holiday shopping. In fact, some people choose to start shopping as early as January, when last season's leftovers are priced at their lowest. Many stores try to lure customers in with promises of savings up to 90 percent. Their main objective, of course, is to make way for next year's inventory. The big problem with postholiday shopping, though, is that there isn't much left to choose from. Stores' shelves have been picked over by last-minute shoppers desperately searching for gifts. The other problem is that it's hard to know what to buy so far in advance. Next year's hot items are anyone's guess. But proper timing, mixed with lots of luck and determination, can lead to good purchases at great prices.

Hacker/Sommers, Exercises for A Canadian Writer's Reference,
7th ed. (Boston: Bedford, 2019)

EXERCISE P5-1, page 75

a. As for the advertisement "Sailors have more fun," if you consider chipping paint and swabbing decks fun, then you will have plenty of it.
b. Correct
c. After winning the lottery, Juanita said that she would give half the money to charity.
d. After the movie, Vicki said, "The reviewer called this flick 'trash of the first order.' I guess you can't believe everything you read."
e. Correct

EXERCISE P5-2, page 76

In his article "The Moment of Truth," former vice president Al Gore argues that global warming is a genuine threat to life on Earth and that we must act now to avoid catastrophe. Gore calls our situation a "true *planetary emergency*" and cites scientific evidence of the greenhouse effect and its consequences (170–71). "What is at stake," Gore insists, "is the survival of our civilization and the habitability of the Earth" (197). With such a grim predicament at hand, Gore questions why so many political and economic leaders are reluctant to act. "Is it simply more convenient to ignore the warnings?" he asks (171).

The crisis, of course, will not go away if we just pretend it isn't there. Gore points out that in Chinese two symbols form the character for the word "crisis." [or crisis.] The first of those symbols means "danger," and the second means "opportunity." The danger we face, he claims, is accompanied by "unprecedented opportunity" (172). Gore contends that throughout history we have won battles against seemingly unbeatable evils such as slavery and fascism and that we did so by facing the truth and choosing the moral high ground. Gore's final appeal is to our humanity:

> Ultimately, [the fight to end global warming] is not about any scientific discussion or political dialogue; it is about who we are as human beings. It is about our capacity to transcend our limitations, to rise to this new occasion. To see with our hearts, as well as our heads, the response that is now called for. (244)

Gore feels that the fate of our world rests in our own hands, and his hope is that we will make the choice to save the planet.

EXERCISE P6-1, page 77

Although I am generally rational, I am superstitious. I never walk under ladders or put shoes on the table. If I spill the salt, I go into frenzied calisthenics picking up the grains and tossing them over my left shoulder. As a result of these curious activities, I've always wondered whether knowing the roots of superstitions would quell my irrational responses. Superstition has it, for example, that one should never place a hat on the bed. This superstition arises from a time when head lice were common and placing a guest's hat on the bed stood a good chance of spreading lice through the host's bed. Doesn't this make good sense? And doesn't it stand to reason that, if I know that my guests don't have lice, I shouldn't care where their hats go? Of course it does. It is fair to ask, then, whether I have changed my ways and place hats on beds. Are you kidding? I wouldn't put a hat on a bed if my life depended on it! [or . . . on it.]

EXERCISE P6-2, page 78

a. A client left his or her [or a] cell phone in our conference room after the meeting.
b. The films we made of Kilauea on our trip to Hawaii Volcanoes National Park illustrate a typical spatter cone eruption.
c. Correct

d. Of three engineering fields—chemical, mechanical, and materials—Keegan chose materials engineering for its application to toy manufacturing.
e. Correct

EXERCISE P7-1, page 79

November 2, 2017
To: Patricia Wise
From: Constance Mayhew
Subject: Express Tours annual report

Thank you for agreeing to draft the annual report for Express Tours. Before you begin your work, let me outline the initial steps.

First, it's essential for you to include brief profiles of top management. Early next week, I'll provide profiles for all managers except Samuel Heath, whose biographical information is being revised. You should edit these profiles carefully and then format them according to the enclosed instructions. We may ask you to include other employees' profiles at some point.

Second, you should arrange to get complete financial information for fiscal year 2017 from our comptroller, Richard Chang. (Helen Boyes, too, can provide the necessary figures.) When you get this information, proceed according to the plans we discussed in yesterday's meeting. By the way, you will notice from the figures that the sale of our Charterhouse division did not significantly affect net profits.

Third, you should email a [or the] first draft of the report by December 11. Of course, you should proofread your writing.

I am quite pleased that you can take on this project. If I can answer questions, don't hesitate to call.

EXERCISE P7-2, page 80

a. Correct
b. The swiftly moving tugboat pulled alongside the barge and directed it away from the oil spill in the harbour.
c. Correct
d. Your dog is well known in our neighbourhood.
e. Roadblocks were set up along all the major highways leading out of the city.

EXERCISE P8-1, page 81

a. Assistant Dean Shirin Ahmadi recommended offering more world language courses.
b. Correct
c. Kalindi has an ambitious semester, studying differential calculus, classical Hebrew, brochure design, and Greek literature.
d. Lydia's aunt and uncle make modular houses as beautiful as modernist works of art.
e. We amused ourselves on the long flight by discussing how spring in Kyoto stacks up against summer in London.

EXERCISE P9-1, page 82

a. Correct
b. Some combat soldiers are trained by government diplomats to be sensitive to issues of culture, history, and religion.
c. Correct
d. How many kilograms have you lost since you began running six kilometres a day?
e. Denzil spent all night studying for his psychology exam.

EXERCISE P9-2, page 83

a. *MLA style:* The carpenters located three maple timbers, twenty-one sheets of cherry, and ten oblongs of polished

Hacker/Sommers, *Exercises for A Canadian Writer's Reference,*
7th ed. (Boston: Bedford, 2019)

Answer Key   **AK-9**

ebony for the theater set. *APA style:* The carpenters located three maple timbers, 21 sheets of cherry, and 10 oblongs of polished ebony for the theatre set.
b. Correct
c. Correct
d. Eight students in the class had been labelled "learning disabled."
e. The Canadian National Vimy Memorial in France had 11 285 names inscribed on it when it was unveiled in 1936.

EXERCISE P10-1, page 84

a. Howard Hughes commissioned the *Spruce Goose*, a beautifully built but thoroughly impractical wooden aircraft.
b. The old man screamed his anger, shouting to all of us, "I will not leave my money to you worthless layabouts!"
c. I learned the Latin term *ad infinitum* from an old nursery rhyme about fleas: "Great fleas have little fleas upon their back to bite 'em, / Little fleas have lesser fleas and so on *ad infinitum.*"
d. Correct
e. Neve Campbell's lifelong interest in ballet inspired her involvement in the film *The Company*, which portrays a season with the Joffrey Ballet.

Basic Grammar

EXERCISE B1-1, page 85

a. stage, confrontation, proportions; b. courage, mountain (noun/adjective), climber, inspiration, rescuers; c. need, guest, honour, fog; d. defence (noun/adjective), attorney, appeal, jury; e. museum, women (noun/adjective), artists, 1987

EXERCISE B1-2, page 86

a. his (pronoun/adjective); b. that, our (pronoun/adjective); c. he, himself, some, his (pronoun/adjective); d. I, my (pronoun/adjective), you, one; e. no one, her

EXERCISE B1-3, page 87

a. told; b. were, killed; c. brought down; d. Stay, 'll [will] arrive; e. struggled, was trapped

EXERCISE B1-4, page 88

a. Adjectives: weak, unfocused; b. Adjectives: The (article), Spanish, flexible; adverb: wonderfully; c. Adjectives: The (article), fragrant, the (article), steady; adverb: especially; d. Adjectives: hot, cold; adverbs: rather, slightly, bitterly; e. Adjectives: The (article), its (pronoun/adjective), wicker (noun/adjective); adverb: soundly

EXERCISE B2-1, page 89

a. Complete subjects: The hills and mountains, the snow atop them; simple subjects: hills, mountains, snow; b. Complete subject: points; simple subject: points; c. Complete

subject: (You); d. Complete subject: hundreds of fireflies; simple subject: hundreds; e. Complete subject: The evidence against the defendant; simple subject: evidence

EXERCISE B2-2, page 90

a. Subject complement: expensive; b. Direct object: death; c. Direct object: their players' efforts; d. Subject complement: the capital of the Russian Empire; e. Subject complement: bitter

EXERCISE B2-3, page 91

a. Direct objects: adults and children; object complement: weary; b. Indirect object: students; direct object: healthy meal choices; c. Direct object: the work; object complement: finished; d. Indirect objects: the agent, us; direct objects: our tickets, boarding passes; e. Direct object: community service; object complement: her priority

EXERCISE B3-1, page 92

a. In northern Italy (adverb phrase modifying *met*); as their first language (adverb phrase modifying *speak*); b. through the thick forest (adjective phrase modifying *hike*); with ease (adverb phrase modifying *completed*); c. To my boss's dismay (adverb phrase modifying *was*); for work (adverb phrase modifying *late*); d. of Mayan artifacts (adjective phrase modifying *exhibit*); into pre-Columbian culture (adjective phrase modifying *insight*); e. In 2002, in twelve European countries (adverb phrases modifying *became*)

EXERCISE B3-2, page 93

a. Updating your software (gerund phrase used as subject); b. decreasing the town budget (gerund phrase used as object of the preposition *in*); identifying nonessential services (gerund phrase used as subject complement); c. to help her mother by raking the lawn (infinitive phrase used as direct object); raking the lawn (gerund phrase used as object of the preposition *by*); d. Understanding little (participial phrase modifying *I*); passing my biology final (gerund phrase used as object of the preposition *of*); e. Working with animals (gerund phrase used as subject)

EXERCISE B3-3, page 94

a. so that every vote would count (adverb clause modifying *adjusted*); b. that targets baby boomers (adjective clause modifying *campaign*); c. After the Tambora volcano erupted in the southern Pacific in 1815 (adverb clause modifying *realized*); that it would contribute to the "year without a summer" in Europe and North America (noun clause used as direct object of *realized*); d. that at a certain point there will be no more oil to extract from the earth (noun clause used as direct object of *implies*); e. when you are rushing (adverb clause modifying *are overlooked*)

EXERCISE B4-1, page 95

a. Complex; that are ignited in dry areas (adjective clause); b. Compound; c. Simple; d. Complex; Before we leave for the station (adverb clause); e. Compound-complex; when you want to leave (noun clause)

Hacker/Sommers, *Exercises for A Canadian Writer's Reference,* 7th ed. (Boston: Bedford, 2019)